Praise for ~~Five Courageous Mothers~~

"Anne Tucker Roberts [...] [...]t of five pioneer women wh[...] [...]hil-dren with Down syndr[...] [...]me-changers who made pro[...] [...] with hope and a protective love-in-action to nurture the personal growth of their special needs children. In the process, their children have flourished, and those around them have been enlightened about the inherent worth and unique qualities of every individual, no matter what the intellectual ability. Through these pages, the reader can feel the sadness, the fury, the weariness, the joy and the humor that infuse the lives of those with Down syndrome and the families who love them."

—Florence Lai, M.D. Neurologist:
Mass General Hospital, McLean Hospital, Harvard Medical School

"I entered the field in 1978 as part of the deinstitutionalization movement and development of the community system; inspired by my sister-in-law, Lisa, who had Down syndrome. The stories of these moms stirred strong emotions in me. I was struck by their courage, tenacity and selflessness! They maneuvered uncharted waters, creating more meaningful lives for their children and greater opportunities for those who followed them. Their indomitable strength and commitment were truly inspiring...never underestimate the love and power of a mother!"

—Beth Moran Liuzzo, Area Director
Brockton, MA, Department of Developmental Services

"What a different world raising a child with Down syndrome was during the 1980s and 1990s versus the 2000s and today. Being the father of an exceptional 10-year-old boy with Down syndrome, I have firsthand experience of what is expected in raising a child with special needs. The compassion, determination, devotion, and undying love these mothers have truly inspired me to keep doing what I am doing."

—Jeffry Roback, President Mass D.A.D.S.
(Dads Appreciating Down Syndrome) affiliate of MDSC

Praise for Five Courageous Mothers

"Anne Tucker Roberts has brought to the fore the stories of some incredible mothers and their children (now adults) with special needs whom she has encountered during her remarkable teaching career. The book takes the reader through the journeys of those families – the surprises, heartbreaks, struggles and joys of these remarkable mothers and their equally remarkable kids. This is a book of real courage, true commitment and inspiring perseverance in the face of incredible challenges and pressures (both personal and societal). Parents, educators and healthcare professionals would all benefit from reading this powerful book!"

—Dr. Christopher T.S. White
Licensed Psychologist/ Licensed Applied Behavior Analyst
President and CEO/ Road to Responsibility, Inc.

"This book is instructional and inspirational. As a pediatrician for 40 years, I have been involved with many families confronted with the task of raising a child with Down syndrome. Some have been unable to face the task, but most have, as the families described here. They have met the expected challenges, such as education and social integration, as well as the unanticipated challenges, such as societal ignorance and family conflict."

—Dr. Paul C. Schreiber, MD
(Recognized as Best Doctor in America in 2008)

"For 23 years I served as Executive Director of North River Collaborative, an eight-town educational service agency serving special needs children. I thought I understood the heartbreak and joy that parents of these exceptional children felt, but Anne Tucker Roberts has captured those emotions in a way that is raw and eye-opening. I praise the women who trusted Anne with their very personal stories and urge parents, educators and others who have the privilege of having a special needs child in their lives to read this extraordinary book."

—Dr. Patricia K. Maley, Former Executive Director
North River Collaborative, Rockland, MA

FIVE COURAGEOUS MOTHERS

Raising Children with Down Syndrome

ANNE TUCKER ROBERTS

Anne Tucker Roberts

OMNI PUBLISHING CO.

2018

Published by
Omni Publishing Co.
www.omni-pub.com
May 2018

Library of Congress cataloging-in-publication data
Roberts, Anne Tucker
Five Courageous Mothers: Raising Children with Down Syndrome
ISBN: 978-1-928758-01-3

Printed in the United States of America

Design by: Leonard Massiglia

This book is in memory of my mother,
Mary Elizabeth Hayes Tucker,
who introduced me to courage.

It is dedicated to all women, especially
my sisters, friends and mentors
who embody courage.

Table of Contents

Introduction

I spent nearly 20 years teaching adolescents with Developmental Delays. Each student spent six years with me mastering new skills for adulthood. Along with the students, I worked steadily with their parents preparing them for their child's graduation from school and into adult services. I thought I understood Down syndrome.

But, it was on an ordinary car ride on an ordinary September day that I learned the extraordinary backstory of one remarkable student, Edward. His mother, Hazel, laughed heartily, regaling me with stories of raising him. One story was memorable. When Edward was young, she explained, she would saunter around the living room, dressed as an old lady, creating stories and speaking with an Italian accent while Edward looked on. Why? These antics, she thought, would increase his attention span, while teaching him words. Intrigued, I asked what made her do this. And here was the shocker – a reality about most of my students with Down syndrome that I didn't know. At Edward's birth, the hospital staff and Hazel's family urged her to institutionalize him. They all agreed with the doctor's dismissive comment, *"Down syndromes don't learn anything."* Instead, she took Edward home. It is Hazel's astonishing story of creativity and perseverance that needed to be told.

Other mothers of my students offered to tell me their story. They, too, took their infants with Down syndrome home when families and doctors counseled them otherwise. There was no Doctor Spock for them to consult. "Early Intervention" hadn't been coined and very few in the medical field could even offer "Best Practices" for dealing with obstacles. In fact, a healthy life for their children was a looming question mark.

These remarkable women tell of navigating the world of unknowns with challenging fits and starts. In listening to them, the thread connecting them became clear. These women are the courageous pioneers for services that are in place today. They are the quiet heroes in neighborhoods like yours and mine. They did not carry on about SAT scores or even dresses for the prom. They were not worried about their teen drinking and driving but about them thriving. Meet Hazel, Connie, Lisa, Ann and Jane. Their stories of tenacity and love inspire even the bravest of us.

Chapter One

Hazel Straughn and Edward (Casey)

My son, Edward, was born January 25, 1980, with just one additional chromosome – he has Down syndrome. I was caught unaware and pushed into this frightening unknown. First, you ask yourself, "Why?" Then you think, "Never in God's world am I going to be able to handle this."

The News

In the summer of 1979, I didn't even know I was pregnant. I was 41 years old, soon to be 42 in December. I had stopped going to Dr. Casey, my OBGYN. However, I began having a few problems and missed a period. When Dr. Casey heard this, he said, "Oh, well, we'll see how you go. Maybe we'll do a lower GI test to see if something is wrong, but this is not alarming. You may be just starting 'the change.'"
"Okay," I said.

Soon after, I was on the tennis courts and said to a friend, "You know, I think I'm pregnant. My legs are like cement. I have energy, but I am so heavy feeling." I called Dr. Casey that afternoon on my way to a swim meet for my daughter, Carolyn. He told me to bring in a urine sample and said, "I will know by 5 pm if it is positive."

All afternoon, every chance I got, I was out at the pay phone; I was even calling the office between the swim meet races, ones I was supposed to be timing. I got nowhere. Finally, I reached an operator and pleaded, "I am running out of dimes. I am trying to get my doctor for test results." She put the call through and Dr. Casey answered, saying, "You are 100 percent pregnant." "Oh my God," was my only answer. I thought it would be *my* time now that my two children, Bill (12) and Carolyn (10 going on 11) were in school. I had intended to get a job that fall at, of all places, Cardinal Cushing School.*

Looking back to that year, 1979, I was physically and mentally healthy; I couldn't get more fit – playing tennis every day from May until October. I only gained 17 pounds throughout my pregnancy. Early on, the doctor did mention having an amniocentesis test, but the results would have taken two to three weeks and by then I would have begun to feel life. I quickly dismissed the thought of getting the test and nobody – friends or family – thought anything about this pregnancy despite my age. Down syndrome or any other disability was not on our radar. I joked that this baby was going to be my doctor or my lawyer. My husband, Harry, was teased by friends and renamed "the stud."

After keeping my pregnancy a secret for a month or so, I finally told my children and, with much excitement, they shouted that they wanted twins – one each. That same day, as scheduled, we went to the Swim and Tennis Club and both Bill and Carolyn ran to tell the news to their swimming instructor. She, in turn, went on the loudspeaker and announced," Mrs. Straughn is in a family way." Kids were going home that night saying, "Mrs. Straughn is in a family way. What does that mean?"

We were typically at this club all day in the summer, from nine in the morning until ten at night. After arriving one day, I put our bags and towels on a table and looked down. Blood! I grabbed a big beach towel and went to the phone booth to call Dr. Casey. I told him I was hemorrhaging, and he said, "Get to St. Margaret's. I will head over." I called Harry to tell him to meet me there.

Without even knowing the directions to the hospital, I went off with another mom, leaving Bill and Carolyn with a friend. We ended up lost in Boston's Chinatown. Finally, we stopped a police car. The policeman came over and looked in the window only to see the seat – and me – laden with bloody towels.

*Cardinal Cushing is a living community and school begun by Richard Cardinal Cushing in 1947 for 35 "exceptional" students. Today, students from ages six to 18 are schooled in functional academics as well as daily living, vocational and recreational skills.

"We're trying to get to St. Margaret's," I cried, "but we're hitting all one-way streets and I'm hemorrhaging." "Follow me," he said, and away we went, with sirens blaring. After an examination in the ER, I was admitted and stayed overnight, as this was the critical three-month mark. A nurse came in and asked me how I would feel if I lost it. I said, "What will be, will be. I have no control over this." Everything stayed intact; I was free to go home, and the doctor told me that I would give birth on February 20 – Harry's and my fifteenth wedding anniversary.

Summer turned to fall and soon winter came along. Suddenly, in January, my water broke. Dr. Casey told me to keep my feet up and put towels underneath me; he wanted to keep me from delivering the baby for as long as possible. He explained that no harm was being done to the baby, and that I would be okay unless I ran a temperature. I finally went to St. Margaret's on a Tuesday but went home two days later, after my kids called Dr. Casey to tell him a surprise baby shower – which I couldn't miss! – was planned for that Thursday night. I managed the baby shower sitting on towels. We laughed and carried on. Friday, as I was getting the kids ready to go to school, I started shivering, really shivering. I thought I must have a temperature and called the doctor to be safe. "Get the kids taken care of and come on in," he said. Harry, who was already at work, came home, drove me to the hospital and then left for a basketball game. I was alone, except for the nurses monitoring my contractions.

The Birth

This was unlike either of my other two pregnancies. With those, I went through labor easily, but this experience had me go through waves of contractions. Finally, at 10:30 pm they called Dr. Casey, who came in to examine me, gave me a spinal and told me not to push...just "breathe like a dog." I can still hear myself panting, and in between saying, "I prooomiz...I ammmmm Nooooot Puuuuushhhhhhhhing." Finally, at five minutes to midnight, out came this little baby. I had already told Dr. Casey that I wanted a girl – and I did not want a redhead. When my baby was delivered, Dr. Casey said, "Oh my God, it's a redhead...Oh my God, it's a boy." Right away, this little guy was whisked off to the ICU. I never really saw him; the only thing I happened to see was a little slanted eye.

A resident came into my room shortly after I delivered. I was alone, not knowing anything about my own newborn. He said, "Your

5

son is a mongoloid." I looked at him in disbelief. He was stern and said emphatically to me, "Say it, say it." And I finally muttered, "Mongoloid."

Dr. Casey came in shortly after that, and he and I cried together; just he and I. Harry came in that night, after midnight, despite my protesting, "This is nothing special, it's no biggie. Just stay there with the other two." After peering into the ICU, Harry said to me, "I saw a halo around him. He's special." That was so unlike my husband – I had to take it in.

The next few weeks were hell. I stayed in the hospital for a week, fielding questions from doctors, nurses and social workers. I had nothing to say. At that time, they institutionalized people with Down syndrome; I was given that option. One of the nurses told me that they didn't have to put him in an institution; they could put him up for foster care. She went on to tell me that I did not have to bring him home, no questions asked. I was shocked. Of course, I would bring him home.

I missed meals just to be down in the ICU, where I could sit and stroke his hand. I couldn't hold him, I couldn't feed him, and I couldn't yet take him home. I just talked to him. Even before I named him, I noticed that the sign on his incubator said, "Baby's Name: (Edward Casey) Straughn; Doctor: Edward S. Casey." After asking permission, we named him Edward, but have called him Casey forever.

When Edward was two weeks, he had to be seen by a pediatric cardiologist, Dr. Feingold, who needed to investigate what was apparently a slight heart murmur. He found nothing to indicate anything abnormal, except for a slightly slanted eye. He said, "I don't want to say anything definitive about him, and don't you, until these blood tests come back." We had two to three weeks more to wait; I was a basket case and felt like I looked 92. There were many, many nights I cried myself to sleep. The test results finally came back and, yes, Edward had Down syndrome.

Edward was not floppy like most Down syndrome babies, and his sucking reflex was good. However, he had a lung infection, he was blue, he weighed five pounds and was five weeks early. Because of his infection, they treated him with antibiotics intravenously through his head, and protected the spot they had to shave with a cup – placed on his head like a crown. When my sister came in and saw it, she immediately called him "King Casey." She even went so far as to get a t-shirt made for him that said, "I am the King."

6

After he was home, and I had the freedom to touch him, this whole thing finally became a reality. I thought, "I will handle what I have to handle," but truthfully, I didn't know anything. At night I would be downstairs where my children couldn't hear me, hysterically crying to the point of not being able to catch my breath. "Why me?" I'd ask, "What have I done?"

I was also in and out of fits of anger – angry that this happened to him...and to my other two children. His disability would put such a responsibility on them; I worried how much Edward would interfere with their lives.

Acceptance

I was so, so scared for a very long time. With friends, I used to joke and say, "I tried to put him back, but he didn't fit." I found that – in order to cope – you joke a lot and you lie a lot.

I am not one who sits in church, but I do have "Holy Mother Mary" icons around the house for comfort. It was at Easter time, the year he was born, around two in the morning. I was feeding him and lost in my own world, just thinking. All of a sudden, I felt this sharp pain, a very sharp pain in my back; it was excruciating. Strange, but at that moment I thought, "The Holy Mother knows this pain," and "this is what will help me get through it." Instantly, I understood it's not what you can *handle*; it's what you have to *do*. I made the decision then and there – "He's going to make it." The pain subsided, and I have never felt it since.

Early on, I went to a parent group and when I got there I found that the others were all professionals: nurses, pediatric doctors, etc. They knew before they gave birth that they were having babies with special needs. I noticed that Edward was the only one crawling; the others were held close to the parents' chests like precious rag dolls. A few group members said to me, "I wouldn't want my child any other way." Amazed, I replied, "You've got to be kidding me. I would give my arms and legs at this moment to have him be a regular kid." I never went back to that group. I did, however, speak to my pediatrician. "Is there something wrong with me? These parents are going to be psychiatrists. I don't have time. Is there something the matter with me?" "No," he said, "you've accepted the fact." I was satisfied and decided therapy was not for me. That parent group was the extent of "services" offered at the time. There were no programs or people knocking on my door wondering how I was managing.

Our town was a very small place then, and news traveled like wild-fire when Edward was born. Bill and Carolyn were also in the local school system, so all their teachers knew. Along the way, I would have teachers and well-intentioned people say, "You should do such and such." Nine out of ten of them never had kids, much less a kid with special needs. I was getting advice from everyone, and as much as I was grasping for ideas, I would take what advice I thought I could use. The more I talked to people and the more I heard myself use the words Down syndrome, the more I began to accept it.

I was on a mission, as most parents are, but this was different. You go along day by day and do what you can do. I would say to Bill and Carolyn, "He's going to reach for a star, and we're going to push him to it." I didn't know what he could do because I had never been here before. When the light goes on for him, that's what you take. And it does come on.

As for my older children, their lives went on. Before Edward was even born, Carolyn volunteered in an after-school program with students from the Paul A. Dever School, then a school in Dorchester for children with developmental disabilities. These kids were tough; they were explosive. They bit her and threw things, but she grew to understand them. My son, Bill, had a much harder time accepting Edward in his life. It wasn't until he went to college at Northeastern University that he could even say to me, "I love Edward." Edward and he are not only brothers now, they are true friends; the same holds true for his sister, Carolyn.

Milestones

Edward wasn't walking when my other children did, so I found a physical therapist, Mary, when he was a year old. I brought Edward to her home for therapy. To set up for one of these sessions, she and I rearranged furniture; taking the cushions off sofas and chairs, and pulling out tumbling mats, balloons, nerf balls – you name it. We worked on everything: following directions, muscle tone, mobility, coordination, even articulation. Together, we addressed different problems as they arose. The activities we did were all those that a regular child would do, only we did it in smaller steps – slow motion, you might say. "Go get me the banana on the couch." He would have to crawl, not walk as others his age might. He would get to the cushion, climb onto that, crawl up to the couch, climb up onto another cushion, get the banana and then bring it back to me, telling me the word for what he had in his hand. There were two things I was learning in this process: first, I had to make learning playful, and second, I had to plan every move. Just think about what goes into standing up from a chair. Most people would say you simply have to put your feet on the floor and lift, but actually, you bend forward first, and then put your hands on your lap or on the side of the chair. I had to be clear about how to do whatever it was I asked him to do, step by teeny step.

The other thing I remember was his first steps. He walked at 18 months, but he shuffled his feet, never lifting them. I had to teach him to place his heel down first, then his toes. We sang, "Heel-toe, heel-toe" and marched around and around the living room. To improve his muscle tone, we put a bar in one of our doorways and had him do pull-ups and chin-ups. Sure enough, *we* had to do it with him, too. Thank goodness Carolyn and Bill were teenagers, so I was occasionally relieved of "chin-up duty."

Carolyn and Bill would go to their friends' houses, but sadly, they did not bring friends to our house. When they *were* with Edward, however, they were very attentive. Edward was a toy to both of them, one they loved to have fun with. They swam with him, read to him, and played with him frequently.

I would get so gassed up seeing Edward catch on and learn a certain thing. When he finally began walking, we played a game called "The little old lady from Italy." Naturally, I played the little old lady, donning a scarf on my head and talking slowly with an Italian accent. I would send Edward into the living room to pick me up a *meat-a-balla, a loaf-a-bread and a glass-a-milk*. He loved these skits and joined in the make-believe stories. In the spirit of play, Edward learned to imitate all sorts of characters I would make up. Little did I know that these performances were important for what later developed: a keen understanding of adventure, an intrigue with accents, a vivid imagination and a love of books, which still serves him well.

Speech

Edward's memory was getting a good workout, but his speech concerned me. I remember asking a doctor friend of ours, "Where is the vocal part of the brain? Why isn't he talking? He has got to talk!

9

He can't make it if he doesn't talk." "He will be fine," the doctor said. "It's just going to be a very, very slow process.

I didn't want to wait. For a long time, we sat on the floor in front of a mirror with him between my legs. I could see that the whole structure of his mouth needed to move more, and his ability to form words needed to be developed. We started with all sorts of tongue exercises and sang in front of that mirror every day. Actually, we babbled: "La la la la and Beh Beh Beh Beh." We would continue in the car with whatever we were practicing at home: singing our ABC songs, nursery rhymes or songs I remembered teaching my other two, such as "Put One Foot in Front of the Other." Everything we did, whenever we could, was singsong. He began to get it! When he did start talking, at age three or later, telling him to be quiet was not allowed in our house. I told my family to just let him go and when he makes a mistake, correct it on the spot.

To build on this, we took him to Children's Hospital for speech therapy when he was just over a year old. (He loved playing on the elevators and always knew which floor we were going to.) After a number of speech sessions, the staff said there was nothing more they could do for him. He had progressed so much because Carolyn had played many similar board games with him, ones that she made at her volunteer job for students at the Dever School. She brought them home each night and we would sing the directions to him, "Put the pole in the hole…" He had a good attention span, as long as we kept it fun.

As he was learning to socialize, I would tell him, "Don't say 'I am fine,' say 'I am fine and how are you?'" I would again play act. While walking around the living room, all of a sudden I'd turn around and ask, "How are you?" And I waited for his full response. I had to learn to do everything in slow motion; one step at a time, one word at a time, one concept at a time. Constant talking and frequent repeating worked.

We never labeled things in the house. I insisted that if he wanted something, say to drink, he would have to come to me and say the word, "drink." He would repeat it until he said it correctly. I made it clear that he was to use his words with everyone. Whenever he wanted to give up, he was told, "Don't say, 'I can't,' say, 'I'll try.'"

I went to the special education director when Edward was two-and-a-half and asked to enroll Edward in the town's preschool program for children with special needs. (He was potty-trained at two, so I thought he was ready.) At that time a child had to be three but the director said that he could start if I drove him back and forth every day until his birthday. So, from September to January I drove, and after that he was allowed to take the bus. On that exciting, landmark day he popped out of bed and waited eagerly at our back door for his first bus ride.

At one point, early on, I went into his classroom and the teacher began, "This is the signal to go to the bathroom." Immediately, I said, "No, I don't want sign language. I don't want a crutch for him. When he has to go the bathroom at home he will tell me." People seemed to push for sign language then, but I did not want it. Fortunately they listened, and he never had to learn to sign.

First Love – Reading

Having an adolescent boy and girl meant my children were never at the same place at the same time. They were on swim teams and in other sports in town. I had made a commitment to myself that Edward was not going to interfere with their lives. He had to learn to go with the flow, so he got used to eating in the car and going wherever and whenever my others had to go. I always carried a bag of audio tapes; he loved to listen to the Disney stories and would *read* along with them. He got to the point where he could follow the words and turn the page correctly when the tape beeped. He also learned to find the right tape for the right book. I remember one person who, seeing him so captivated, came over to me and said, "You're so lucky he's reading." I had to be honest and replied, "No, he's got it memorized." Wherever we went, the other teenagers were great with Edward. He would go from one to another, and when he got tired of one he would find someone else. They would read to him, talk to him, or play with him. He was never just plopped down somewhere; he was an active part of everyone's life. He learned about other people's feelings and emotions – and I hope they learned from him.

Edward never tired of engaging, and books would keep him occupied for hours. We read constantly in our house. When he was very young, I read to him all the time, stories like *The Night Before Christmas*. I would use my hands to indicate the snow was falling, pinch my cheeks for St. Nick's rosy cheeks, and I would click-clack like the reindeer on the roof. Later, when he'd hear any of the stories, Edward performed every gesture he had seen me do. To this day, he is an astute observer and a great imitator, with a memory like steel.

11

His elementary school started a mega-books series, which I used as his treat at night, as well as his punishment. He *loved* to be read to, but if he hadn't done his homework, picked up his room, or gotten his clothes ready for school, I wouldn't read. I also noticed that so many people indulged Edward and he was starting to get smart with me, so if he was fresh or gave me mouth, I wouldn't read.

As he got older he loved series books, especially *The Hardy Boys*. I would read him a chapter every night. There are 63 books in that series; we read them all at least three times. *Harry Potter* series? Same thing. He knows all the characters and each story. He was so sharp that if I made a mistake reading he'd correct me. These books are still on the shelf in his room – even when I try to help him clean things out, those books don't go anywhere. Just recently he asked me to reread *The Hardy Boys* with him.

Early Life Lessons

Edward knew who he liked and didn't like, and made no bones about showing his dislike. In grammar school, a notebook went back and forth between his teacher and me. One day, she reported: "Today at recess, Edward decided to bang two boys' heads together. I spoke with all three boys but could not come to any reason for this. Edward spoke up, saying 'I just don't like them.'"

Another excerpt from this notebook read: "Today at recess I had to ask Edward to stand by himself at the wall. He had gone up to a boy in the schoolyard and told him to move out of his way. Then, as he walked by, he pushed his classmate down. The boy bounced when he hit the ground. I was concerned about this because he landed only about an inch from the pole of the swings. I reprimanded Edward and he seemed to understand." He needed to learn how to get what he needed or wanted without such physicality!

People, for some reason, loved to feed Edward, constantly. It got to the point where I had to tell well-intentioned people that the doctor put him on a strict diet, otherwise he would be eating all the wrong things. Edward will pick up bad habits quickly. It is easier to learn the bad ones than the good ones, so all bad habits must be stopped immediately. I told most everyone to be strict with him because "give him an inch, he'll take a mile."

Some bad habits were scary. In department stores, he would romp around and then hide underneath a rack of clothes. If there were drawers, he would pull one out and climb in, leaving me searching. One day at our local supermarket, Edward went into the men's room without telling me. As I searched for him, the store went into lockdown and the manager called his name over the intercom. People in the parking lot, many of whom knew Edward, heard the reason for the lockdown and began to holler his name. Suddenly, Edward came sauntering out of the men's room. We learned then that the intercom didn't reach the bathrooms, so he didn't even know we were looking for him. Such fear never leaves me. I decided to try to show him how scary going missing is, so I reversed the scenario and he now knows that hollow feeling of losing me. Even today, he remembers and doesn't let me out of his sight. He has called me over the intercom in all sorts of stores. I could be in the next aisle of the grocery store, but if he can't find me he'll go immediately to the service desk and have me summoned. He has had me paged at the mall, too. I used to take him there and let him go from one store to the next on his own, always knowing where he was and memorizing what he had on for clothes. One time, he went into one store and I walked down to the next store, as I always did. Suddenly, I heard a loud male voice say, "Hazel Straughn, please report to the security desk." Edward somehow didn't see me right outside *his* store, so he went to the security police and told them that I was missing. He uses common sense when he has that sick feeling, so I guess my experiment worked.

Edward has some common sense but his ability to judge new situations is often skewed. Once, a different bus driver met him at school to take him home. He did not get on the bus despite the driver telling him that she was there for him. When he got home, he said, "I did not know that van driver, so I walked straight home."

His common sense is one thing, but he also just doesn't know when to keep his mouth shut. And I learned that the hard way! A doctor's wife was at the Swim and Tennis Club. A large woman, she eyed a lounge chair to plunk down on. As she neared it, Edward cried out, "Oh, no, you're too fat. You'll break it." There is no filter. And P.S. Never tell him that something is a secret; he will quickly spread the news all over the place.

As Edward matured, I set very strict parameters and made it clear that he could do what was acceptable within those guidelines. I never spanked Edward, but had to find effective ways to punish him, when necessary. If he had an attitude or a nasty tone in his voice, I would tell him to go the bathroom and wash his face until it was gone. Most of what I tried worked, but I relied simply on instinct; I really didn't know what I was doing. You come to do things on the spur of the moment – it's not written anywhere. Sometimes you wonder if you did the right thing, and then you agonize. I wouldn't wish this on my worst enemy, but then again, I don't know what my life would have been without him.

Second Love – Swimming and Medals

Edward really grew up at the Swim and Tennis Club because of our commitment there with our two other children. One of the swimming instructors, Fran, would take Edward into the pool and work with him during "Adult Swim" time. He was swimming, thanks to her, when he was five months old. Other club members became interested in him, and he easily went from person to person; he was not special needs in that setting. He never wore a life jacket, and as he got a bit older he would walk around the pool alone. I would respond to people who questioned this by saying, "He knows where his body is; if he falls, he falls. He will have to go down three times before he learns. There are plenty of eyes on him here; he'll be okay." In the neighborhood or elsewhere, whenever Edward did fall, I would say to him, "Don't bleed! Blood stains! Get up and shake yourself off."

Edward was only five or six when he was recruited to participate in Special Olympics. That's a year or two ahead of most athletes. We went to Bridgewater State College for their tryouts, and he came in fourth. In the official, grand style of the Olympics, they announced the names of the winners and had them stand on platforms to receive the gold, silver and bronze medals. It was then time for Edward to receive his fourth-place ribbon. He took it, saying, "Thanks, but I only go for the gold," and promptly threw the ribbon into the wastebasket!

He participated in Track and Field when he was seven and did okay, but Edward's legs have never been an asset; his power is all in his upper body. At that same time, I brought him up to a fitness center to swim and one coach, Kathy, took an interest in him. She had a pool in her backyard and suggested we go there for lessons – and did he learn. She taught him Freestyle, Breaststroke, Backstroke and Butterfly. For years, he swam with regular kids on various South Shore teams, and for ten years he swam with four other special needs kids who called themselves the Sharks – all before he was 16. Edward's forte was Free-style and Breaststroke. Over time, the Sharks – Gerald, Artie, Christian and Edward – were top relay swimmers. They had no competition and swam against the clock.

A group of us parents would host parties and fundraisers for the Sharks. We held a banquet at the Swim and Tennis Club once and raised money to buy Special Olympic sweat suits for the team. Another time, when Edward was nine or ten, we raised enough money to send his whole class and their teachers to Disney World for four or five days. The group took a limo to the airport and then, given a head's up, Jim Green, the "sky high patrol" pilot for Boston traffic announced, "There goes the limo taking the special needs kids to Disney, toot as you go by." Everyone had a ball.

The Sharks continued to do well and went on to swim for the championship. A teammate, Artie, was to swim last. His sister knelt at the side of the pool and whispered her sage advice. "Don't you dare breathe 'til you get out." Finally, when he surfaced, he asked, "Can I breathe now?" They were victorious, beating the national team by a full 25 meters, and were nominated to go on to the Nationals.

Edward swam four or five days a week through middle school. At one of the last get-togethers, when Edward was 15 or 16, his swim mate, Christian, decided to give up Special Olympics and, because they were a relay team, Edward decided to do the same. To this day, when asked about swimming, he says, "Nope, I'm retired."

Medical Traumas and Game Changers

I learned early on that when a child with Down syndrome gets sick, the infection travels fast. My primary care doctor gave me a val-uable tip. "When you call any doctor's office, tell them that Edward has Down syndrome and they will get you in the back door. They know that this population needs attention quickly. Even if it's just a cold, they just can't say "take two Tylenol and call me in the morning." To this day, I still follow that advice.

Edward had terrible stomach aches in grammar school. He would have explosive, often unexpected bowel movements. There were times I would be cleaning toilets at the mall, throwing away his clothes and buying new ones on the spot. It came to the point where he was drink-ing full containers of Metamucil every day. My hunt for a diagnosis was exasperating. One doctor told me to bring in bowel specimens and then sent me off saying Edward just had an intestinal bug. But something was clearly wrong. His stomach would expand – literally rise way up – and then he'd shout, "Mom, I gotta go, I gotta go." He would burst with stool, black stool. Carolyn and I finally brought him into Children's Hospital. They sedated him and did a multitude of tests, even taking a biopsy of his intestine. Their diagnosis? 100 percent lactose intolerant. That is when we began Fiber Com and quit all dairy products.

I still give him Lactaid milk and he checks with me all the time if a new food is in the offering. He will simply forego eating if he is not sure or if he knows he hasn't had a lactose pill. Before all of this he ate most everything; now he is extremely cautious. Even I have made mistakes in my choices of food for him, which has made him even more leery of trying new things so he sticks to safe foods. Five mornings a week, before school – or now work – Edward has a bowl of Reese's Puffs, 9 ounces of Lactaid milk, some juice and, after he showers, a Diet Coke while he watches his show on TV. On weekends, he will have a bagel, bacon, juice, milk and, of course, his caffeine – a Diet Coke. For lunch every day, Edward has a dinner roll, 4 pieces of thinly sliced bologna, a bag of chips, a banana, and a container of sugar-free lemonade. Every night he has two low-sodium hot dogs with ketchup, a large, no-salt, soft pretzel and a mug of his Lactaid milk. Later, he'll call out for his snack – a sugar-free ice cream sandwich. He eats less than he used to and never eats between meals.

As a youngster, Edward didn't eat soft foods; he always had to have things that were hard and crunchy. He is now eating salads here and there, consisting of raw green beans, cucumbers, lettuce and celery. We tried carrots, but he once got a few bitter ones, so they were out. It has taken years, but I finally have a variety of foods to feed him: cans of lite fruit, sugar-free ice cream, pretzels, Fudgicles, Klondike bars, sugar-free Jell-O, and pudding. His diet is much better than it was, but it's boring, and odd.

Going out to eat is a challenge. Once, a group of us went to a restaurant on the water in a summer community. I asked for a hot dog for Edward and they said they didn't have any – only hamburgers. I had to get in the car, drive to the grocery store around the corner and buy a package of bologna and a bag of pretzels. "I am sorry," I said to the waitress when I returned, "but you don't want me to sue you; he is allergic to what's on the menu."

When Edward was young, doctors would automatically test his urine for sugar. It's always been on the high end, but I thought it was because he had usually just eaten something prior to the appointment. When he got to high school, however, the school nurse mentioned that he was cramping up, drinking a lot and always going to the bathroom. There were reports that he was also sleeping all the time on the van going back and forth from home, out to worksites and even on field trips. He was also moody in class and seemed generally disinterested.

I tried to piece together timely incidents that I thought might have influenced this. For one, his good friend from the gym had a seizure on the basketball court and died in front of him. It was very, very emotional. That year, there was also a bad flu season and Edward was hit by it. And lastly, I attributed these mood swings and the little he did complain about to his sleepiness. We finally took him to a psychiatrist to evaluate his moodiness and low energy. After an hour with him, the doctor said, "There's nothing wrong with this kid."

It was hard to sort through, but his symptoms, including stomachaches, frequent urination, insatiable thirst, tiredness, dizziness and complaining that he couldn't see, did not get better. At a routine appointment at Children's Hospital, the doctors were alarmed to discover he had dropped 35 pounds – pounds nobody noticed because of the baggy sweatpants he wore at home and to school. They ran blood tests and told us they'd call with results in two days but phoned just 24 hours later. "He has diabetes," they said. They told me later that I could have lost him.

Edward was admitted into the hospital for a few days and was put on intravenous insulin; I slept in the chair in his room. A personality clash got in the way of his treatment there, so we headed to the Joslin Diabetes Center in Boston. Even though he was 20, we went to a pediatric unit where all insulin was premixed. We learned about diabetes quickly. Edward was taught to do his own testing; I would do the mixing. From the beginning, we have kept a running list of his sugar levels, five times a day, if not more. People with Down syndrome have a tendency toward diabetes, but in Edward's case it is inherited from his father's family.

What does this mean? It means I can't send him for four or five hours anywhere. I can't have people take him to a movie because he shouldn't sit that long. Unless I go along, everyone is afraid he'll have an episode of going high or low. Being sedentary will drive his sugar levels up; too active, he'll go low. That's why I travel with all sorts of snacks. Water is a constant, it's a filler, and walking is the best thing for him. However, nothing is a sure bet. He can go to the gym at 3 pm, work out, and have high sugar levels at 5 pm. There are no two people the same, and there is no telling day to day what will happen. That makes most people uncomfortable.

The good news is that Edward knows what to do; however, he needs constant reassurance. He carries sugar tablets in his apron every day to work; he has candy in his lunch bag and his tester is always on him. He might call me after he eats lunch to tell me he's low. Calmly, I ask if he's had lunch and eaten his banana. If he has, I tell him he's okay. He needs to know that he did the right thing. I still wait until noon every day to know if he is all right before I can be relieved from running to his work to give him a shot.

Edward is comfortable with me because it's always been the two of us managing this. When Edward was in the hospital, newly diagnosed with diabetes, Harry wondered why I was staying in there with him. What he really wondered was "Who is going to take care of me?" Later, when the visiting nurse came to teach us how to do Edward's insulin, she called out, "Well, come on out here Harry, so you can learn." Harry replied, "Oh no, I'll do what I have to do when I have to do it." To this day, 18 years later, he has never learned nor helped with any of Edward's diabetes issues. He doesn't bother to know his diet, his schedule or his routines; he's just here.

I make a point to educate Edward's drivers, his managers at work and the staff at the gym about Edward's diabetes and what he is capable of doing independently. I am adamant that he eats the food I pack every day, and that he exercises at the health club most days.

Edward has been at this gym, Health Fit, for some time. Originally, when he was swimming there, they gave him a locker and a lock. He would put some clothes in one locker and some in another, and then he would misplace the key. "I need your help!" he would shout from the locker room. They cut off more locks until they finally decided that his gym bag would be better off left at the front desk. And, despite the changes in management, Edward's clothes remain behind that desk.

With the diagnosis of diabetes, staff at Health Fit put him on the treadmill for a certain amount of time and then onto circuit machines.

In the beginning, they printed out his program and I would take it to the Joslin Center where they reviewed it and either said, "Fabulous, keep it up," or adjusted it. He tests himself the minute he gets to the gym. If his sugar is high he is told immediately to go walk it off; if he is low they give him orange juice or candy. Then he calls me. "I'm low, Mom." I just say, "Okay." I have complete peace of mind when he's at the gym. His work place offers the same comfort. If his sugar was low at 7 am, I know what he will be eating and, therefore, I know he will be in good shape. If they call me worried, I tell them he is fine, just fine. I am that confident.

I can open the door to Health Fit and instantly know what machine he is on because I can hear him singing. I have told the staff that if he gets too loud, tell him to pipe down. "Oh no," they say, "it puts a smile on our face!" Edward is hooked on watching General Hospital at 3 pm, and one of the other people at the gym likes watching the Food Network while he's working out around the same time. The two of them were always trying to get there first to put on their show. The health club realized this and now they schedule one show on one channel, and the other show on another. Both now walk the treadmill happily!

School Trials

It was at Health Fit that I met a math teacher from a Vo-Tech (vocational-technical school) who put new hope in our lives. He encouraged me several times to put an application in for Edward, telling me, "Edward's got the ability to do this. I will speak up for him." In those days, some of the students at the Vo-Tech were not the brightest academically, but they could all read and write; Edward could not. The Vo-Tech had an advertisement that said, "We don't discriminate against special needs." I thought, okay, we will try. We took it to the next level and met with both his middle school special education teacher and the town's special education director. We hired a lawyer affiliated with the Department of Developmental Services because Edward was the first "handicapped" person applying for placement at the school. Our attorney encouraged us, saying, "This would be breaking ground for those who could handle it." I was thrilled; Edward would be learning a trade!

To make this work, three parameters were established: Edward would be tried in various vocational settings in the school; the town would hire an aide to be with him at all times; and his previous middle school teacher would supply the appropriate academic materials. Edward was so enthused to start in September, and after opening day things went along okay for a while. Soon, however, the administrators began putting stipulations in place. For example, I was restricted in my interactions with his aide and his teachers. I was not allowed to talk to them one-on-one; all discussions had to happen with Edward's "team," which included his teachers, his aide, the principal and the special education director.

Rules were strict for Edward too. He rode the Vo-Tech school bus, but when he disembarked he was told to sit on a bench at the entrance and wait for his aide to get him. Rules like this made him feel like an oddity. Unlike all the other students, Edward could not go to his locker or walk the hall on his own. All that training in independence from his grammar and middle school years was for naught. Further, it was decided that if Edward's aide called in sick, the school would call me and Edward could not go to school that day. Many of his rights were violated.

Academic classes suffered as well. Math consisted of being handed colored paper clips to count; and teachers or his aide would read to him instead of having him continue to learn to read. They did not invest any time to make this work.

He came home one day and told me that he had detention. When I asked why, he said, "They were calling me names on the bus, so I went to the office and told them." "Well, that's high school stuff," I replied, "You'll have to get used to it." His detention, I later learned, was because he caught onto those not-so-nice words and used them to retaliate against his bus mates. He also figured out a hand "sign language" and became proficient at when to use it. Kids were always turning him in for that. I got a call another time and was told that he had been in the men's room rubbing feces all over everything, including the walls. Through the aide, I learned that incident was not done by Edward. A lot of hazing was going on; staff and kids were turning everything around to implicate him.

Teachers and administrators simply did not want him there. The Vo-Tech put him in Culinary Arts, but instead of varying his jobs they stuck Edward at the sink alone, cleaning huge pots and pans using scalding hot water. Usually, two students were assigned to this job and they would rotate cleaning and drying. Not when Edward came. He was segregated, included but not included – pure discrimination!

The pace was just too much for him; he couldn't keep up, but he kept quiet – never a word to me. The aide would call me at night and let me know the truth of what was going on.

At this same juncture, I was trying to plan for Carolyn's wedding. The chaos around preparing for her big event and managing Edward's schooling, especially given my inability to talk to any teacher when incidents came up, became too much. When there were meetings, there were no positive reports. The "team" made you think that they knew better, they evaluated things better, and they were in charge – period. Slowly, they were trying to get him out of there, and even began telling me that they didn't have the facilities or the staff for someone like Edward.

It was a hell zone for me from September until April, but after spring vacation I said, "Enough," and called the school to tell them he would not be back. I don't remember any of Carolyn's wedding in May. I was in a size five dress, down to 129 pounds. I was having a nervous breakdown and I was anorexic. Shortly thereafter, Edward said to me, "Thanks for taking me out of there, Mom." In all those months, I never heard, "I don't want to go to school." Never. It was hard on him, but he didn't show it. We thought that if he could make it through the Vo-Tech, it would be an important breakthrough and would give another child with a disability the chance to attend. It might even have opened the door to specialized vocational training for this population, but that was not going to happen and, to this day, has not happened.

I had been in contact with Edward's middle school teacher, keeping her apprised of what was going on. When I returned Edward to her classroom after spring break, it was clear that the only immediate goal for Edward was to reassemble his shattered self-esteem.

I have never been back to the Vo-Tec. To this day, I have never received anything from them: no records, no papers – nothing. Edward doesn't even look that way when we drive by it. It's a memory, one he doesn't forget.

Third Love – Movement and Dance

For the most part, Edward has been asked to try everything a regular kid does. Early on, we tried roller skating and then roller blading. He just doesn't have the ability. He can't ice skate either; all he did was cry when we tried. We even bought figure skates for him, thinking they have more support in the ankle. It was just not there.

We have gone coasting on a golf course in a nearby town. He loves to go down, but when he gets to the bottom he yells, "I need help." I would run down and then have to lug the coaster back up. He would like to snowboard, but I don't think he has the ability no matter how hard I push; it's a balance issue with Edward.

Edward rides a bike but knows he is only allowed to ride in our cul-de- sac. We bought him a bike when he was ten or 11; it had heavy-duty training wheels made to hold his weight. He came home from school one day and said, "I want the training wheels off." Carolyn and I took one wheel off and ran holding his seat. He was wobbly and un-able to steer, but all of a sudden, he pedaled off screaming. Within three days he rode without any training wheels. Edward loves to go fast on the bike or the sled, but he's not thrilled with roller coasters. He'll tell you he's afraid of heights, but he's not afraid on a plane, nor was he afraid at the top of the Eiffel Tower.

The only thing Edward has asked for was a driver's license. At first I gulped, but then got the manual for him and handed it over say-ing, "Now you have to read it and learn it." "But I need your help!" he exclaimed. "You don't help me drive, I can't help you," I replied. "Well, you have to come in with me." "No, I can't. The policeman will be there with you, not me. You have to take the test and he will tell you if you passed." That ended that. He has never asked again.

Aside from riding a bike and swimming, Edward loves to dance. Years ago, we went to a party and Edward was down on the floor doing twirls. People were looking at him saying, "Look at him, he's funny." With Carolyn getting married, I decided to give them something to look at and became determined to find him proper instruction.

We began dancing lessons with Denise at her studio in Abington. Today, thanks to her, he can do the Waltz, the Fox Trot, the Cha-Cha, the Mambo, Swing, the Rumba and even the Tango, his favorite. He has been doing this for 13 years and is completely comfortable on his feet. There are 13 steps to the Tango, and each requires not only know-ing which way to go, but also what to do and when. Denise titled every step for Edward: the Basic, the Diego, Sneak, Della Cruz, España, Me-rengue, the Switch, the Chair, the Mask, Grape Vine, Tootsie Roll, Sombrero, and the Rocking Step. She simply tells him which one is next, and he is able to do it. It takes at least two Tango songs, or about five minutes, to complete all the steps. He has an excellent memory and is smooth on his feet.

I found Denise after calling a few places. When I called a well-known dance studio, I told them that Edward has Down syndrome. Quickly, they replied, "Oh, we are not insured." I think that is what scares people off, but I am always up front about it. One day, Carolyn and I just happened to drive by Denise's studio and on the spur of the moment decided to stop in. She didn't hesitate, and so began weekly classes. Edward leads perfectly, holding Denise, with her eyes closed, his hand fixed in the middle of her back. When he makes a mistake, they stop. "Sorry, I'm tired," he'll say.

Edward likes being *the* show. He tends to zone out when he's on the dance floor, and surprisingly he doesn't get distracted by anything around him. Denise has tried to throw him off; she will switch songs to make him think of what dance step to do, and has even mixed up where they start and where they finish just to change things up a little.

He has been asked to come to her other classes and demonstrate for them. He has done solo recitals; they've done performances for the Plymouth Association for Retarded Citizens (PARC) and made an instructional video of themselves dancing. His coordination, his balance and his sense of timing have become extremely good. He walks like a duck but when he dances, his feet glide gracefully across the floor.

Fourth Love – Music and Girls

I've never known what developmental age Edward really is and, truthfully, I never have figured him out. Edward lives incident to incident, not day to day. When a much-waited for Miley Cyrus CD was about to come out, it was all Edward could talk about for weeks. The clerk in the store told us it would be available on the thirtieth of the month. Edward asked, "Well, how many more Tuesdays is that?" and went to the calendar to count. We were first in line. For hours, he listened to it and danced all over the house but then he took it to the gym. I thought he would show off there, but instead he began twisting and dancing to the Chipmunks. Yes, he goes from Miley Cyrus to the Chipmunks.

The show *High School Musical* irritates me to no end. If I could get a hold of Ashley Tisdale or Miley Cyrus, I would shake them for thinking they are such *big* stars. They don't even bother responding to their fans one of whom, to this day, is Edward. After that movie came out Edward couldn't get enough of these girls and was desperate to get in touch with them. In his weekly call to his Uncle Donny in Florida,

Edward revealed these heart throbs and Donny listened, encouraging Edward's truly blind romance. Soon Edward began dictating letters to Donny to be sent to Ashley and Miley. The following is an actual letter sent by Edward:

Dear Ashley,

I am sending you a picture of myself in my tuxedo. I am more than just a fan, I am the one who got you guys in the newspapers. Will you send me a picture of you?

Your fan,
Edward

No acknowledgement has ever come, leaving Edward so frustrated. Once Donny printed a picture of Ashley and sent it to him. Poor, wishful Edward took it upon himself and wrote on it, "Casey, thank you for buying my CDs," and then he signed *her* name. One of the things Edward succeeded in doing, despite not being able to read, was to look up the email address for Ms. Tisdale in one of the teen magazines he scoured in a store. He then dictated an email to his Uncle Donny to send to her – all to no avail. He gets an A for trying.

He has called the Boston Disney Station, 1160 AM, and asked to talk to the stars because, for some reason, he truly believes that he's the one who has put these girls on the map. Why he thinks this I don't know. The person on the other end of the phone always tells him, "Well, you'll have to call back later." They can sense that there's something different about this particular caller, but they don't have the nerve to hang up on him. The funnier thing is that to call Disney you have to be 14 years old or younger. Edward knows this and knows he is too old, but has figured out that he can use his younger niece's name and her birth date. I told him it was against the law to call and give someone else's name and age to get a gift or win a prize. He says he will do it until his niece reaches 15, which fortunately is this year.

Edward loves to learn the words to new songs, but he can't read the lyrics insert because, for one thing, the font is too small. He is quite savvy and has roped in certain people to google the words and print them in a larger font. With all sincerity and in his theatrical style he tells them, "I've *got* to learn this song!" He also asks them to print a duplicate copy, "for Mom," in case he loses his. Lyrics in hand, he will sit in his room with the door shut, his earphones on, singing at the top of his lungs. He can't sing as fast as the singers do, so for a while he just gets the last few words of each line, but he persists until he masters it. He has hundreds of song lists and I have thousands of pages of lyrics.

Edward also wants to learn the dance moves to these songs and is constantly writing for the "steps."

Dear Miley,

Do you know your steps to your "Hoedown Throwdown" dance? Could you send me a copy of the steps that you do with your choreographer and on your DVD? Thanks.

Your fan,
Edward.

The same entourage of people he has printing his lyrics are also hooked into looking for his steps online. I would love to leave a tape recorder in his room. He is his own best friend in there, carrying on various conversations and always getting the answers he wants! Whether he's talking to a music idol or a movie star, he's in seventh heaven, laughing uproariously and even talking back to them.

Edward can't get enough of movies. He can watch them over and over to the point where he knows all the dialogue. I think in a way he becomes these people. He comes downstairs once in a while and talks to me as one of the actors. He loves *Mash*, for example, and identifies with Hawkeye. He'll come to me saying, "I need my Martini."

As he has gotten older, his hormones have kicked in and girls are much more interesting. When I went to his room once to check on him getting ready for work he pulled the shower curtain back a bit and said, "Mom, I am a man trying to take a shower!" I have told him that it is all right to use his room for his "private business" and he knows that. Everyone is to knock before they enter.

One time, my second cousin, Dave, walked into the family room only to see Edward with his arm around my niece's daughter. He was rubbing and kissing Alyssa's shoulder. Dave called his wife, Vicki, who in turn yelled frantically, "Ha-zel!" I said, "Okee-dookee" and called Edward to my room. We sat down to another talk. "Those actions

25

are not appropriate," I said. "She is your cousin. You can give her a hug and a kiss on the cheek when we come and when we go. That is IT. HANDS OFF GIRLS! You want to do your *thingee*, you go do it in another room or the bathroom. You know the rules now. And furthermore, you do not walk up to a girl and say, 'Hello, how are you? I want to marry you.'" Edward thinks girls are going to fall in love with him right away. I tell him that you have to be friends with a girl for a very long time. You have to talk on the phone, bowl together, go to a movie and get to know each other. After all this, he says, "I am going to make the best dad ever." Supposedly he is 99.9 percent sterile. I have no proof and don't want to try to find out. Even with his sister and her girls, there is no sitting on laps. All I have to do is look over at him and he'll say, "I know the rule, Mom."

Despite knowing what is expected, he always says in his deep actor's voice, "I need a wo-man!!" A classmate, Martha, was a girlfriend once. He invited her to a Halloween party. Apparently, not long into the evening he left her. He did not stick to her like a date might have; instead he was flitting all around. He didn't really get what being on a date was all about. When asked how it all went, he replied, "She dumped me!"

He is a constant surprise and through adolescence has kept me on my toes. I never know what or who he'll be interested in next.

Adult Life Lessons

I always tell people that I can only get sick from ten at night until six in the morning. If the legs are working, I am *on*.

For Edward, it is very scary if I'm not well. When I had to tell him that I had breast cancer, he was devastated. He went to my radiation appointments with me. Before the first treatment, I had to have an EKG; he didn't want to leave the room and said, "I'll just stay here, Mom, and won't look." He sat in a chair in the corner, put his coat over his head and remained like that the entire time. Knowing a little about cancer, Edward hated when I smoked. Whenever I lit up a cigarette, he would say, "Oh, here goes Dopey having her sanity stick!"

Edward has been through a lot of life and death situations. He can handle it. He knows what a wake is and what death is; he also knows that death is permanent. He will go to a wake, hug you and tell you he's sorry. The next day, or the day after, thoughts come back and often he is sad for a while. My brother, whom he was very close to, died in

December. I told him that Uncle Joe has gone to heaven; he is up there with Grammy and Grandpa, Great Grandma and Grammy Martin. He seemed okay with it that night. He went to work the next day and I got a call that he was bawling uncontrollably; it just hit him. When I picked him up, he got in the car and cried like a baby. I asked him why all the tears, and he told me his uncle died. What I told him then, as I had years ago, was that God put us here. "He's the chief and when He decides it's time, He's going to bring you home so you won't be sick anymore."

He'll look at the picture of our dog, Tiffany, who was our best "babysitter." Tif would get into the playpen with him and later slept right by his bed. She was always between Edward and whoever else was here. She would never bite, but if you moved and got up she would growl. Edward knew she was there to protect him. She is buried out in our backyard; Carolyn's dog, Nicky, is in the front yard. Edward, from time to time, will go outside and sit there talking to them both. He can be emotional; tears coming and going in spurts. You never know what he is thinking, ever, even today.

I taught Edward to say prayers when he was little and always told him, "God hears children before he hears us adults. You talk to him; he'll keep an eye on us." Edward still says his prayers every night. He does not recite, "Now I Lay Me Down to Sleep" or the "Lord's Prayer," but starts off with, "Hey Pal." He includes the whole family: siblings, parents, grandparents, even the dog. He also adds people he knows who are sick, and people he wants kept safe like his brother, Bill, who travels a lot by plane.

Edward is so programmed. Each night he goes upstairs, brushes his teeth, gets my nightgown out and lays it on my side of the bed, and then goes into his room. He gets into bed halfway. I go in, pull up his sheets, and then he puts the radio on. Every night I ask him, "Did you say 'em?" He answers, "Not yet." I remind him of those who need a few extra prayers and then leave the room. He calls out, "You forgot to give me a kiss goodnight." As I leave a second time he has to ask if there is a storm coming; he cannot take thunder or any noise in the night. I walk down the stairs and hear him begin, "Hey Pal." He ends his prayers with a line he memorized for his acting debut as an angel in a middle school Christmas play: "Glory to God in the highest and on earth, peace and good will to all men." He has said this every night since he was six years old.

The Essence of Edward

Edward cares about people. Our neighborhood had a lot of kids when Edward was growing up. One family next door had six children; Tommy was Edward's age. When Tommy invited his school friends over he would sometimes include Edward, but Edward would fall behind when they went into the woods and they would forget that he was even with them. Edward would have only made it to the other side of the brook in our backyard before he began calling out for me, but he'd go with them the next day again if they asked. Other neighborhood kids would always say "Hi" to him, but because his summer days were spent at the Swim and Tennis Club, there wasn't a lot of interaction. Edward, however, liked to think that *he* looked after the neighborhood kids. Once, he warned some of them not to ride their bikes off the black top because he had just been chased by a hoard of yellow jackets.

Another neighbor had a pool, so many of us gathered there often. One of the other fathers in the neighborhood was so good to Edward that I would introduce him to newcomers as Edward's *other* father. Edward touches people. You have no idea who or when. And Edward doesn't even know the extent.

He was always close to my brother and to his teacher Anne's husband, John. When Anne and John took Edward's class to New York City one year, Anne's dad also became special to him. One story he likes to tell people is how Anne and John ran him into McDonalds in New York City when he was so sick with a stomach bug. He has never, never forgotten and says, "They were so good to me." Another endearing person was Jim. He was the dad of Christine who was on Edward's swim team, the Sharks, for years. Jim often took the two of them to events and rooted Edward on. Edward to this day says, "Jim treated me like a son."

When Jim got sick, I would go and clean his house and Edward would visit, sitting by his bed. Edward still talks to him every time we go by the cemetery. I don't know what the specific influences are, but certain things and certain people he does not forget. You don't have to do a lot with him, just spend a little time with him.

Despite his aggression in grammar school, Edward fortunately outgrew having to bang heads to get his way and has grown into a person who gets along well with others. He had no problems in high school with other classmates, and now has no personality problems with his manager at work or fellow employees.

Edward can be kind and thoughtful. As a reward for being a ten-year employee at Stop and Shop, he was given a catalogue and told to pick out a present for himself. He picked out fresh water pearl earrings for his niece McKenzie, who at one time irritated him to no end, but whom today he loves like a sister. He has also taken to calling his sister, Carolyn, every night just to check in.

As thoughtful and sensitive as Edward is, he also has a definite stubborn streak. He is a manipulator. Things have to be done Edward's way and in Edward's time. For example, he wanted to thank people recently for their birthday gifts. I bought the cards and he sat at the kitchen table dictating each letter. He signed them and said, "We'll mail one at a time." I said, "Well, I will put them in the mailbox as I go by tomorrow." "No," he said, "One at a time. I got the presents one at a time, we'll mail these one at a time."

Edward also likes his things arranged the way he likes them and, despite it appearing disorganized, he can find most everything he needs in his room. He does not like it when I suggest cleaning in there. One day when he heard Anne, his teacher, was dropping by, he told me he didn't want to go to work. He hounded me, asking, "What is she coming for?" I told him that Anne was coming to ask me some questions. He persisted, "What about? Are they about me? Are they about picking up my room? Are you going to show her my room?" Keep in mind, he will not pick up anything if he can get away with it.

The other part of this streak is that we go where Edward wants to go – *his* stores and at *his* pace. We poke at Wal-Mart in their electronics section, but we don't go to Wal-Mart's woman's department or housewares, even if I need something. We go to the music store in the mall and he'll say, "I'll just look around," and I stand there. Sometimes employees have gone to the back room to get me a chair while Edward is still looking around.

Edward can try your patience. And one day he did. Driving home on this day, I slammed on the brakes and I told him to "GET OUT. You have pushed me to the limit; get out of this car." He knew I meant business and he cried. But he learned. Not much later, in middle school, when he was asked to do something, he turned around to his teacher, Laura, and said, "Ms. Breault, you have pushed me to the limit." Incidentally, he was not a saint at school all the time either. Once, he was sent to the hallway for something he did in the classroom. While there, he noticed that all the lockers had color-coded padlocks. Mischievously, Edward decided to change the colors on all the locks, except for his own. Nobody, but Edward, could get into their locker that day.

What does he do with disappointments? He will pout and stomp, and with tight lips in an angry, frustrated voice he'll say, "*MO-TH-ER!!!*" I ignore it now and say, "I don't like that – get rid of that tone. He goes to his room (what he calls "his living quarters") and gets over it. He can also get an attitude if he doesn't get his own way. He will cross his arms, put on a sour face, complete with furrowed eyebrows, and become testy. The theme one year for a Halloween party in middle school was *Snow White and the Seven Dwarfs*. You'll never guess who Edward wanted to be – Grumpy. How fitting! What you see is what you get. He does not know how to cover his reactions, even if it gets him into trouble. At the same time, he will take the shirt off his back and give it to you if you ask.

Harry

My husband, Harry, has patience for every other young person – even those with special needs – but not for Edward. From the beginning, Harry was too involved with his own life, saying, "I have to do this or that," or "I have to go here or there, so have dinner ready because I have to be out of here." He has always been self-absorbed.

For some reason, Harry has never been able to use the right tone of voice with Edward. I have learned that you cannot talk to Edward with a temper, nor can you show tension because that stresses him out. Harry and I can't even have an argument when Edward is home; Edward will walk outside the house and I won't know where he has gone. So, no matter how mad I am at Edward or how frustrated I am at what he has done, he does not go out the door without a kiss and an "I love you" from me.

Sadly, Harry has never been able to show much affection for Edward. Even as a youngster, Edward used to say, "I want to give you a hug goodnight," and Harry would push him away saying, "No, I don't want a hug." Harry might not be a hugger, but when you have kids, especially one with special needs, you just have to do it.

It's odd, but Harry has been to several dinners for the "Best Buddies" program (students who take special needs kids under their wing). He sees the loving interactions these people have developed – how much they have given and how much they have gained. He seems proud of *those* special needs kids, yet he is still unable to give Edward the love and attention he craves. I have to bite my tongue.

Harry coaches youth basketball in Brockton, but can't make it to Edward's baseball games or weekly bowling events. It's hard to explain, but everyone who knows us knows that Harry simply tolerates Edward. Yet, to this day, if Harry is sick, Edward is the first one there to comfort him.

But now, Harry is actually trying to build a connection with his son. I'm afraid, however, that his new efforts are a little too little, and a little too late. I wonder why he waited so long? He is starting small, doing things like taking Edward to the gas station or asking him to go for a walk. Edward says "No" to the walk because Harry moves too fast. Harry does not know enough to slow down for Edward, but I think he would for someone else's child.

A big part of the problem is that Harry has not learned Edward's world. If Edward needs something, or if anything goes wrong, he comes to me immediately. But if I am not around and Edward asks his father for help, Harry says, "Go call Carolyn, or call your mother on her cell phone; I can't leave right now." He would rather not be bothered and expects someone else to handle it instead. On one occasion when Harry did go to pick Edward up following an event, the supervisors wouldn't let Edward leave with him until Edward finally spoke up and said, "That's my father."

But, when Edward does the good stuff, Harry is there to take a bow. Harry has always made a point of going to Special Olympics because, in that venue, Edward is a star. Harry enjoys the recognition and likes to share the credit for his son's successes. Harry tells co-workers at the office about his Down syndrome son, but he tends to exaggerate his role in Edward's life. I get angry and embarrassed about Harry's inability to have a good relationship with Edward, and I'm not optimistic about it improving.

High School Training and the World of Work

Edward's high school years, from ages 16 through 22, were spent in a substantially separate program learning not only various vocational skills in actual work settings, but also corresponding adult responsibilities and behaviors. At first, Edward balked in his "King Casey" style. He felt above many of the tasks, such as sweeping, cleaning or serving.

At home, he was fine letting me, "Mother," perform all household chores including making *his* bed. Once, while making his lunch, I said to him, "Edward, you could be doing this yourself." He replied, "Well, if you weren't here I would, but you are here." Then he sat down. His teacher Anne, in his high school program, quickly stripped him of his crown and, through behavior charts and verbal praise, Edward began to see the benefits of growing up.

In the summer, his program consisted of paid piece work in the morning followed by a woodworking class in the afternoon. He was picked up early from home and left off at the high school before the program began. Edward would find a bench and promptly fall asleep. For the first few days nobody woke him, but others in the class commented, "How come Edward is sleeping? He can't get paid if he's sleeping." Sure enough, staff docked his pay. I pointed it out when the check arrived. "See, you can't sleep and get paid. No workie, no money!" For some reason, that registered with him.

Edward has been employed as a bagger at Stop and Shop for nearly 14 years. His first job coach after high school took him to various stores in the local mall to fill out job applications, but nothing came of that. When a Stop and Shop opened nearby I took him in to fill out an application. He was hired right then and there, and the same job coach came back to work with him for about six weeks. With that guidance, Edward learned the *right* way to bag food and, equally important, learned the Stop and Shop employee rules, including those about break time. However, after the job coach left, Edward, on occasion, resorted to his conniving ways. One day, for example, he followed protocol at first, asking his cashier for a break to go to the men's room; but she soon wondered what was taking him so long. The boss went to look for him and found him in the book aisle reading magazines. When it happened a second time, management handled it right then and there with a verbal reprimand. The day he was hired, I told them not to give him that inch, and now they don't. He can manipulate any of us and, on those days, I tell him, "If anyone stole you, they would call and pay me to take you back."

Work is now automatic for him. I reinforce that he must do his job and do it right, "otherwise they will fire you." I often repeat our mantra: "No workie, no money." He knows exactly what he is supposed to do and where he is going. If things change, however, he must know ahead of time or he can become frantic. Every day he is up at seven, gets his insulin and continues with the rest of his morning routine: breakfast, shower – you can tell he is showering when you hear the water running along with loud sighs of *Ahhh* and *Ooooh*. He dresses in the clothes he laid out the night before and finally has some caffeine: his diet soda. He is now all set to go, since the night before he put a hanky and his Acucheck in one pocket, cough drops and spray sanitizer in another, and a bottle of water in his gym bag. He is gone by 9:15 – as long as everything has been put in the right place.

Adulthood – New Challenges and Regression

People say Edward is what he is today because I pushed, but I only did so because he had the ability. My goal was to keep him busy all through his school years, so I made sure he got to the gym, dance classes and bowling on weekends. Now, he continues to bowl once a week and he is still a fixture at the gym, but dance has ended for him. Through happenstance, however, Edward began horseback riding lessons a year ago. When he met his instructor and two of her horses, Mia and Summer, things seemed to click. Each week, entering the stable, he immediately starts talking to his "pals" and continues to chat them up while he strokes their necks and brushes them. Edward is used to wearing shorts or sweat pants but those would not do for riding; we had to go out and buy all the gear – the jeans, the boots, the shirt and the helmet. He has been taught exercises to do before he mounts the horse and sits erect in a Western-style saddle. He walks and trots the horses as Shannon leads them. He has been in two shows for beginners, meriting two ribbons. One of the show requirements was to pass by the judges, tilt your head and give a wink. He loves putting on his spiffy outfit – especially the cowboy shirt – and once, as we were leaving for the show, asked, "Am I the main attraction?" One of the onlookers said, "He looks like he has ridden for years." Wouldn't you know, he is center stage at these events.

Edward still needs routine, but he does not need a clock or a calendar. He can look in the mirror on a Wednesday night, for example, and say, "I need a haircut." He knows every fourth Thursday – one of his days off – we go to the barber. Order and predictability in his days assures him that all is well with the world.

I really don't know what to do now that he is 38. He is not able to go to a football game, he can't go to the movies, and I guess, I'm the one feeling guilty that there is nothing for him to do. Sometimes we go down to Star Land and hit a bucket of balls. It's embarrassing that it's just him and me. But I am sure he is not the only one in this boat.

His isolation might be part of the reason he has regressed in some things. Money, for example, doesn't register with him correctly. His Uncle Donny sent him $50 for Christmas. I reminded Edward of the amount when he was about to thank Donny in his weekly call, only to hear, "Hey, pal, thanks for the five bucks." Back in the day, he learned to count money by recycling cans. He turned his nickels in for dimes and quarters, and eventually could count up to a dollar. He can't do that anymore. When he was in high school, he and I planned a trip to England to see his brother, Bill. Edward became obsessed with finding recyclable cans, even telling Ellen, his bus driver, "Mother said that I have to save the soda cans to pay for the ticket." He truly thought that. Edward continues to save for vacations and Ellen still saves cans for him. When he gets his paycheck, we cash it at the bank. Right then and there he takes out the quarters and the one dollar bills, then, in his cavalier style – a nod of his head and a roll of his eyes – he says to the teller, "Give the rest to the 'cheap skate.'" And off he walks. His change and his dollar bills go into his top drawer for "vacation." With his stash of cash, I hear him tell people that he has money "out the ying yang."

From his paycheck, he is allowed one treat a week, that's it. He will buy a DVD or a music CD. People try to spoil him. I finally had to put my foot down with his Uncle Donny who likes to buy him things, saying, "Don't *buy* Edward. Edward gets to buy one thing a week, that's plenty. If he doesn't have enough money, then he can't have it."

When we plan a vacation to see relatives, he can't wait to go. He looks forward to fishing with one uncle in Oklahoma. He learned to cut worms in half and then says, "hook 'em up." He will spend hours casting out for catfish. Other times he looks forward to the swimming pool, but from suppertime until bedtime it is down time for him, no matter where we go. So, when he is asked, "How was your vacation?" he answers, "All I did was watch television." He might have been busy the entire day but all he remembers are his endless nights. He does sit down and play board games or cards, maybe Fish or War, but only to a point.

This is all new – his age of adulthood – a place that I have not been in before but am surely in now. At this stage, it is getting tougher to keep him occupied. He works hard three days a week. The nights after work are not too difficult to fill, but when it comes to his days off,

I hear, "Well, what are we going to do tomorrow?" Those days, if I don't keep him busy from 6 am until 9:30 pm, he will say, "I am bored out of my tree." If he were in a residential home, there would be people interacting with him. Here, he is withdrawing.

I have called a nearby group home in an effort to link him to activities and people he knows, but I get little information back and other agencies that do offer activities are very expensive. The ARC (Association for Retarded Citizens) offers classes but they don't interest Edward. Go and learn hygiene? He's done it. Sex ed classes? He's been to them. Cooking is hardly relevant or exciting and Arts and Crafts classes are not his cup of tea either. I would love to get him back into swimming; it would be great for his diabetes and his skin, but now he plays when he swims.

Edward would probably do more if he had someone close in age with similar abilities, but this social vacuum has a lot to do with his odd diet, the restrictions from diabetes, and people his age who seem to have tough speech impediments. A dance is scheduled for the spring, but he is not that excited. To begin with, he sees that others don't know how to dance; he also can't eat what is put in front of him and he can't stay out until 11 o'clock unless I come with his insulin. He is very aware of what he is, and yet he is choosey about who he interacts with. He doesn't need much; you don't have to spend money or take him to fancy places – just an hour with someone makes his day.

Reflections

It's obvious that I have been the mainstay here 24/7. Harry went to work; I imprisoned myself and I am still there. I do not go anywhere without Edward; that is the bottom line. He is at work with people I trust and then at a gym where I am completely confident staff will treat him well. I can go any day from noon until 4 pm and have peace of mind. But, leave him with just anybody? I couldn't; panic would set in. I would not even leave Edward here, alone with Harry, because of his diabetes. I could leave him with Carolyn or Bill, but not Harry.

Raising him is a job. It's full time and it's exhausting. Edward will never be my lawyer or my doctor or even take care of himself. I have found that in the past, and even now, I can always find a reason not to go somewhere or do something. Maybe I use him as an excuse, but Edward is my priority. Edward thinks it's funny when I tell him he is my third leg. I am always leading, but there he is walking right behind me. His life, his entertainment and his health all come before mine; but he would not know that.

We are compatible, but when I do something he doesn't like he'll say I am an itch with a "b." One day, I got so mad at him I let loose and said, "I am going to put you in a home." "You're never going to put me in a home, are you?" he practically begged. As angry as I get at him, I have to reassure him that he is here to stay. I tell him that I am sorry. "I lost it. You pushed me to the limit." I could never put him in a home; it would break *his* heart, not mine.

Some days you just want to hide away, but you can't. You have a responsibility. If *you* don't do this, who will? I can't escape but I can get engrossed in cleaning a room or working in the yard. There I can leave for a few hours, mentally. You take care of anyone you love. Having kids means they are always a concern; the only difference is Edward is full time.

Edward is considered moderately high functioning – there are others who are even brighter and I do get envious of them. There are many days when I feel as though I did not do enough. I think, "I should have done this; why didn't I do that?" Then you have days when you just wonder where your life would have gone, what direction? I have no idea. I have always thought that there are things in life that are meant to be, and some things you cannot control. I was born at a certain time and on a certain road. I was not meant to be a nurse or a teacher and, for some unknown reason, I was meant to have Edward. From day one, when he finally succeeded at something, it made it all worthwhile.

He was meant to come right here, to this house, whether it was for Bill or Carolyn, or even if it was just for me. Hopefully, my grandchildren will get what it means to have Edward in the family. He has touched everyone in my extended family and brought us closer even though we are in different states. I look at other special needs kids and their parents and wonder, "How can you *not* spend the time? How can you say 'I'm going away' and just put your child somewhere?" I see that being with Edward every step of the way has benefited him. I have to keep telling myself that Bill and Carolyn are going to take care of things. I worry, you don't know who is going to end up being here with him when he needs someone. It's the unknown, again. I can only pray that he will always be treated with respect and dignity.

Chapter Two

Connie Cronin and Jimmy

Innocence

I grew up with lighthearted Disney movies: *Snow White*, *Cinderella* and *Sleeping Beauty*. I cannot carry a tune, but I remember walking through the cornfields in the Midwest singing all sorts of Disney songs, convinced that my "Prince Charming" would ride up on that beautiful steed someday, sweep me off my feet and take me away. As a young woman, I thought this Disney picture had become a reality, only to watch it unravel and crumble bit by heartbreaking bit, finally falling away.

I came East to go to college and met my "Prince Charming" in March 1969 at a St. Patrick's Day Parade in South Boston. Jim took my breath away. He was confident, handsome and so much fun. He was it; I never questioned it. I was bound for a job in Germany, so our courtship had a near two-year hiatus. When I returned, in 1971, we fell in love again, married and bought a house.

Cracks in the Fairy Tale

We entertained often and never passed up an opportunity to go out with friends. The emphasis on partying didn't allow us to build the emotional intimacy and balance we would need to face the challenges ahead. Priorities were skewed, jobs were lost, maturity was delayed.

Three years into our marriage, my son, Jimmy, was born at 7:53 pm on September 2, 1975, at a suburban Boston hospital. He was adorable with a shock of straight, black hair. As he was handed to me, he yawned right in my face. I looked at him, laughed, and thought, "this is so cute," but I was alarmed at how distant I felt from him. Shouldn't I be feeling more? I still had this illusory fantasy that once the baby is put into your arms, the three of you would become that wondrous family, connected on a level that nobody could ever touch. Emotionally, however, things were not matching up. This was new and off putting, so peculiar right from birth.

After Jimmy was born, I was moved to a hospital room with three other women. Those mothers were given their babies to nurse, but I would not be given Jimmy that night. I was told that he was jaundiced and needed to stay under lights. This was unsettling news. I cried seeing the other mothers with their newborns, but it never registered that anything was seriously wrong. I resigned myself to simply accept that things had to be done this way – especially after hearing from nurses that this happens – so I lay there and waited.

The following morning, Jim came into our room and reported that there was a group of doctors around Jimmy's bassinet. With a thousand percent seriousness I replied, "It's probably because they are amazed at how cute he is." "Well, he looks Chinese; his eyes slant," my husband commented. "He has your mother's eyes," I replied, having an answer for everything.

Later that morning, after Jim left, staff brought Jimmy to me to nurse but then whisked him away. My pediatrician, Dr. Kruell, was on vacation, but the doctor filling in for him came and stood in the doorway. He asked if there was a Mrs. Cronin in the room. Not budging, he went on, "I am Dr. Spitz covering for Dr. Kruell. It seems we have a problem. We strongly suspect that *it* has Down syndrome." The other three mothers tried to look away. I could sense this was a concern but honestly, I didn't even know what Down syndrome was.

In my naivety I asked, "Can't we give him some medication or a shot? Certainly, something can be done about this."

Dr. Spitz looked at me sternly, "You're not understanding. Down syndrome means profoundly retarded, mongoloid."

I knew the words: "mongoloid," "profoundly retarded," "jaundiced," but nothing was registering hearing them together.

Dr. Spitz stood fixed in the doorway like a robotic toy soldier. He never came to my bedside, never closed the curtain around us and never touched me. Instead, he turned around to leave saying, "We will be getting back to you; I'll send a nurse in."

I tried to figure out how to reach Jim at work. (This was long before cell phones.) Several nurses had now come to tell me they agreed that Jimmy probably had Down syndrome – they noted he had the Simian crease.*

My obstetrician finally came in. He offered immediate relief, saying he did not believe Jimmy had Down syndrome. "They often make mistakes," he said, "There is a blood test that can be done to confirm this." I so wanted to believe my obstetrician; why wouldn't I? He had known me through nine months of this pregnancy. I held on tight to his thread of hope and began to relax. Jimmy was finally brought to me but did not nurse very well. Finally, Jim came in after work. Excitedly, I told Jim about the obstetrician's "educated" opinion and dismissed Dr. Spitz; after all he was not our pediatrician. "He doesn't know what he is talking about," I said.

From the delivery room, I had called my parents in Chicago telling them that they had their first grandson. They were making plans to come East. Jim's parents and his sister-in-law came to my hospital room that second night to say hello, but both Jim and I just sat there. They could not understand why we were not jumping for joy. We had no idea what to say.

Fears and Tears

The next morning, my pediatrician was back. He came into the room and pulled the curtain around us. "Down syndrome is not the issue right now. He has a duodenal atresia meaning the food he takes in has nowhere to go. There is no opening from his stomach to his intestines." I asked, "Well, can we make one?" "This would require surgery," he said, "but we would not do it on a child with Down syndrome. The quality of his life doesn't merit it."

He went on to tell me that it would be best if I did not go to see Jimmy in the nursery. Further, he would make sure that Jimmy was not brought to me. "With this kind of blockage Jimmy will die in a matter of days. It would be too difficult if you were to get attached." If I was mixed-up earlier, I was utterly thrown now. It was shortly thereafter that I was made to feel even more alone – they moved me to a private room. Now I was scared.

*A Simian crease is a single crease across the palm as compared to two creases in a normal palm.

This snowball of confusion was quickly gaining mass and momentum. When Jim came in, I pleaded with him to call everyone and tell them not to come to the hospital, this was too much to take in. Instinctively, I knew Jimmy should not be alone down the hall without his mother, so I waited until Jim went home and the nurses left me alone. Quietly, I sneaked down to the nursery where I finally held him close. I was 26 years old, I needed time to think; all I could do was rock the two of us.

The next morning Jim told me that he called his close, childhood friend and priest, Billy Joy, and told him about Jimmy. Billy dropped everything and drove to the hospital to christen Jimmy before he was to die. My storybook image of a christening – the celebratory atmosphere, the gathering of the entire family and the flowing, white gown was reduced to the four of us in a hospital room, me in a johnny.

Before Jimmy was brought in, I begged Father Joy, "What am I going to do? They are telling me to let him die. This doesn't feel right." In his calm, kind manner he answered, "Connie, you don't need to make all the decisions for the rest of your life right now, you need to listen to your heart."

Somehow, his presence and those words gave me a chance to take a breath. At the same moment, however, I could see a radical shift in my husband. Right then and there, Jim shut down emotionally; I saw him withdraw. He was *enormously* sad – we both were, but he could not move forward. The next 20 years was like watching a photograph of my husband fade.

Father Joy, seeing the light in my husband's eyes go out, placed Jimmy in Jim's arms. Even though *I* wanted to hold him for his baptism, I remember looking at Jim as he held this baby. This was not what he ordered. Jim wanted an athlete. Period. His world had changed; he lost his footing and I did not know how to help him. He stood there, eyes fixed on Jimmy, and cried. I had never seen Jim shed a tear and I would never see another one. I felt he was saying goodbye to Jimmy and to our "happy-ever-after" marriage. I cannot tell you why, but I knew Jim was not going to be there for me; I was in this by myself. Funny, but I was not confused about this; it was clear as day.

They sent me home to stay on bed rest and kept Jimmy in the hospital. I called my parents to tell them not to fly out, but they were on their way. The next day I lay on the living room couch overhearing my parents and Jim's parents on the deck. They were fighting about whose family this Down syndrome came from. Both wanted to emphasize that it was not on their side. Still tired, very confused, and reeling from this tumultuous experience, hearing them argue made me think, does it really matter? We have it in our family now.

Sometime during the afternoon, a nurse from the hospital called to tell us that Jimmy had a bowel movement. This now meant that his diagnosis changed from a duodenal atresia to a duodenal stenosis which, according to them, meant that "he wouldn't die within two days, it would be more like two weeks. "Don't worry, we can dispose of him," she said. Crushed, I asked how he would die and was told that he would starve to death.

Another phone call came later that night. Gail, one of the delivery rooms nurses softly said, "Mrs. Cronin, you have an option – send Jimmy into Boston. They will save his life without even thinking about it." Immediately, I called Dr. Kruell and demanded Jimmy go to Boston. When Dr. Kruell got the Boston ball rolling, I frantically said to Jim, "You follow the ambulance, you're going into Boston with Jimmy." Hope trickled in, but to make matters more upsetting, my parents kept saying to me, "Don't have the surgery, please don't go through with it." Jim's folks didn't say much, but I knew they opposed it too.

It was late that night when our new doctor, Dr. Murray Feingold, met my husband and the ambulance at Tufts New England Medical Center, Floating Hospital. He sat down and spoke with Jim. "Down syndrome is not a terrible thing. These people have very viable lives. They do well, they contribute to society." Jim came home all fired up. He sat on the floor by the fireplace fixated on the fact that he was told, "Jimmy may even play sports." I remember feeling such sadness for Jim because he could not see the big picture through his fog. I felt another door shut and a bond break and that never changed. I didn't mention this moment of clarity to Jim, ever, because I realized that was just the best he could do. I saw clearly, though, just how it was going to unfold. We would go on as a couple, but I knew I had to gear up and summon whatever I might have inside to do this. It was then that, somehow, I fell completely in love with Jimmy. I decided to schedule the operation.

The day of Jimmy's surgery, I was on the phone with my older brother, Bob, whom I adored and who had previously been my biggest champion. His first words were, "Connie, I don't want you to go

41

through with this surgery for Jimmy." "Please don't say that," I said, "I need you." "Don't do this. It is going to change your life. You're young, you can have other kids."

In those days, the operator clicked into your line telling you that there was a call waiting. I ended my conversation with my brother and took the call from a Dr. Frank. This new voice was very curt. "This is Dr. Frank. I am scheduled to do surgery on your son. I have to tell you that this surgery is completely out of line." "What do you mean?" I queried. "This is an unacceptable risk," he said, "an unacceptable use of medical facilities, money, personnel and time on something that should *not* be considered. He is profoundly retarded." I replied, "Dr. Frank, you *do* that surgery and you *save* his life and I will meet you in your office after the surgery with my husband." "This is against my medical advice." "I don't care!" I said, never thinking to find another surgeon.

On the day of the surgery, Jim and I went into the hospital despite the fact that I was supposed to be on bed rest. I sat down in Dr. Frank's plush, deep, leather chairs to wait. He finally arrived, saying the surgery went well. "Now, I have papers for you to sign." "Papers?" I inquired. "Yes, papers to make your son a ward of the court." I asked, "Why would I want to do that?" I had no idea what he meant, it sounded like Perry Mason to me.

Gazing up at pictures of grown children on his wall, he pointed to each one, saying, "Look at him, look at her. You will have none of this if you don't put him in a state institution. You can go on to have other children."

"Nobody said I *can't* have other children," I replied. He came back emphatically, "They will be so ashamed of their brother. Would you want a brother who couldn't even stand up, who was drooling, who couldn't talk, couldn't be toilet trained?" "Who said that would happen?" I asked. I didn't know if people with Down syndrome could be toilet trained. I simply didn't know anything. My mother had told me that she thought Jimmy would be in a crib permanently and that we would have to get specially made cribs for when he was older. Now the doctor was confirming this. I blurted out, "I am not signing those papers." "Then," he said, "I will see you in this hospital every week of your life because he is going to have problem after problem after problem."

42

I was furious, but try as I might I could not ply myself out of the lavish, leather chair because I was so sore from the episiotomy. I finally pleaded with Jim, "Get me out of here!" and turned to Dr. Frank, saying, "I am *not* speaking to you anymore." We closed the door and went to see Jimmy. Afterwards, I stood on the sidewalk, in front of the hospital waiting for Jim to bring the car around. I was crying so hard that my knees gave out from under me, so I simply sat on the pavement nearly convulsing. A woman pedestrian came up to me and asked, "What can I do for you?" I said, "Just hug me." She did. This was three days after Jimmy's birth. Exhausted, sore, confused and alone, I realized nobody was cheering me on.

In September, Jimmy had the surgery. He came home in the beginning of November. Shortly thereafter, he got an infection in his wound. Could it be that Dr. Frank's prediction would be true? It started to seem that way. Poor Jimmy would come home for a day or two and then spike a temperature and go back in; he would come back again and something else would happen. To have him home for an overnight was a treat.

Help was available for Jimmy through the visiting nurse, but we had to opt out of the service because he was never home long enough. However, there was a nurse who came to the house one time. Jimmy was back in the hospital, my sink was overloaded with dirty dishes and I was in my bathrobe feeling very sorry for myself. I had pneumonia, so staff would not let me in the NICU. This nurse took one look at me and told me to sit down. She looked me straight in the eyes and said, "It's going to be okay." I will never forget those words, never! That is when I told myself that if I get the opportunity, I would pass that message along to other new mothers of babies with special needs. I do not remember her name or what she looked like; she never came back again. Just those words spurred me on that day. (Close to two years after Jimmy was born, I did volunteer at hospitals to talk to mothers who had just given birth to babies with special needs. I would take in a scrapbook of Jimmy at birthday parties, at Christmas, at cookouts, playing softball, etc. It was sad to still hear mothers say, "But, my pediatrician told me not to take him home, to give him up for adoption." I tried to show them the other side.)

With Jimmy newly home one November day, I was giving him a bottle when he started to turn blue. I grabbed the phone and called Dr. Feingold. (I called him often and seemed to always be able to reach him. He later said that he could never forget Jimmy Cronin because half the grey hairs on his head came from him!) Dr. Feingold said, "Oh my God, I am going to get you to cardiology, hold on." I waited a short time and then a voice said, nonchalantly, "Oh, it's probably that hole in his heart." "Hole in his heart?" I shrieked. "What hole? Nobody told me he had a hole in his heart. I have a baby home with a hole in his heart?" "Yes, we thought we could wait until he was two to have it repaired; he must be in congestive heart failure." Imagine, I am holding this baby who is now in congestive heart failure and Jim was out of town.

I scrambled to drive Jimmy to a Boston hospital, where he was admitted to be stabilized. I spent all day there and returned to find Jim home. He asked, "Where's Jimmy?" I said, "He's back in the hospital." This is how it went. He would be home for two hours, or a day, and then right back in. There was so much happening in so little time that to talk about it took longer than it took to happen.

This time they could not stabilize Jimmy. Surgery was scheduled three times but he kept spiking a temperature. The head of pediatric cardiac surgery finally performed open heart surgery on December 29; Jimmy was just four months old. Before this operation, the surgeon called us up to his corner office with big, beautiful windows all around. I began, "Before you open your mouth, I am going to tell you something. This is *my* son, this is *my* baby, and we are committed to him. Do not say anything to me about going to extraordinary measures to save his life. Do you understand?" He said, "It never occurred to me to say that to you, Mrs. Cronin." Instantly, I fell in love with him. I then told him what Dr. Frank had done. He advised me to report it all to the Board of Directors and asked if I would be okay appearing before the Board if it was necessary. I said I would appear before the hospital's president. (I did write that letter a bit later and learned shortly afterwards that Dr. Frank was no longer practicing. Instead, he was teaching, of all things, patient advocacy at a prestigious university in Boston. If I had listened to him Jimmy would be dead.)

Jimmy was in surgery for eight or nine hours. Jim and I sat without a word. At one point, a nurse came out and said, "It doesn't look good; he is not putting out urine. It is not good." Time inched along until finally the surgeon came out. All I saw was his mask; I tried desperately to read his eyes. He pulled the mask down, smiled and said, "He put out urine." A nurse later remarked, "Until today, I have *never* seen this doctor smile in the operating room."

However, he went on to say, "Mrs. Cronin, don't get your hopes up. Sewing that patch on your son's heart was like sewing it to hamburger meat. There is nothing to hold it. In a day or two, I suspect, the patch will pull off and the results will not be good." I asked, "How will we know?" The surgeon said, "His lungs will fill up with fluid and then he will die. The surgery itself was successful, but his heart tissue isn't ideal." I truly believe that, then and there, God helped me. I looked at this man with new strength and said, "He's going to be fine." Jim and I finally left the hospital; it had been a long day.

Jimmy was put into intensive care after this major surgery. I was allowed to go in for only five minutes every hour just to look at him. "No touching," I was told. For 55 minutes at a time I sat in the waiting room on a wooden bench, next to an amber ash tray, smoking and waiting for the next five-minute interval to see him. I filled that ashtray every day. Each time I saw Jimmy I felt as though I was witnessing a crucifixion. They had him strapped down on a wooden cross. He was intubated and he cried, but there was no sound. It ripped my heart out; I could not touch him, much less hold him.

Over the next few days Jimmy's lungs collapsed two or three times, and the nurses would come out saying, "This isn't good. We have to tap his lungs. He won't survive this." I said back, "Yes he will, yes he will." I never doubted it. When Jim would come into the hospital after work, the nurses would say, "Make your wife go home." "I can't make her do anything," he'd reply. I never thought of going home. Being near Jimmy in the hospital was all I knew to do. I left my house in the morning and came home well after dark. My preoccupation got bad. The electrical company shut the lights off in our house because I didn't pay the bill. I have no idea who was taking care of our dog; it was not me.

Until Jimmy was 18 years old, there was not a year that went by that I could get through December 29 without crying, without dread, and without mourning. I couldn't share those feelings with anybody especially as he got older; the trauma was palpable.

Jimmy finally came home in February, still so sick. Back in December, we had gotten a real Christmas tree and Jimmy's presents still sat under it. By February, the tree limbs were practically bare and when you walked by it, needles in the shag rug crinkled under our feet. "This tree is staying up," I insisted. "This is Jimmy's first Christmas, and we are not moving it!" That February day we sat and opened his presents and, yes, one was a baseball mitt.

I do not remember ever talking with Jim about how we were doing. I never asked him how he was, and I never even wondered how I was. I was not cooking or taking care of the house; I was barely showering. I kept declining; I lost weight and smoked too much. Jim was concerned mostly because not taking care of me meant not taking care of him. He was so detached – he wanted his old life back; *his* idea of being husband and wife where we were simply a couple who went out for dinner and had fun. Neither one of us was terribly mature at this point, but when the rubber met the road, somebody had to grow up.

Jimmy was back at Tufts with pneumonia within four days of our February Christmas celebration, and then he went back in March where he stayed for nearly a month. Each day I visited I grew more petrified of encountering Dr. Frank, so I would hide behind the laundry cart even though I knew Dr. Frank could see Jimmy's name on the chart and knew I had to be there. Once, I was so nervous I hid in the broom closet.

More Medical Troubles

When Jimmy came home at the end of March he had a good run. I made plans and flew to Chicago in June with him to see my folks and introduce him to everybody. Jim stayed back to work. We were out there for two days and Jimmy ended up in the emergency room in Aurora, Illinois, four times. There was something wrong with his gut. All night I watched him; it looked like he was having labor pains. The movements in his stomach were sporadic; he would clench, double over and then scream. There was a distinct rhythm to it, which I tried to explain, but the doctor, who happened to be a friend of the family, kept saying, "There is nothing wrong with him, nothing." I would plead, "Dr. Stein, I know this kid, something is the matter. I think it's appendicitis." He insisted, "Babies don't get appendicitis."

The next morning, Jimmy began to vomit green bile. "Forget Aurora, take me to Chicago, now," I said to my father. We raced with Jimmy in my arms into St. Luke's Hospital. (This was before there were infant seats.) My father drove and my mom was in the back seat. I couldn't rant and rave, all I could think to do was to pray. So I closed my eyes and said prayers over and over again. Suddenly, I felt a hand on my shoulder and heard a voice saying, "It is going to be okay." I turned around assuming it was my mom, but I found her sound asleep with her hands on her lap. "Mom did you touch me?" She answered with a reply I already sensed – "I have been sleeping the whole time." With such a new calmness inside, I knew it had to be God and knew then that Jimmy was not going to die. I always believed in God and had rudiments of faith, but until Jimmy, I didn't think God was really there for *me*. I know now that it takes pain and suffering to strengthen and grow faith. Jimmy provided me with the sound foundation for the compelling faith I have today.

We got him into the ER where he was immediately whisked away. The diagnosis? Jimmy had a gangrenous intestine because his appendix had, in fact, wrapped around his bowel. Had it burst, the doctors informed me, he would have died within minutes. The doctor then said we had to do surgery immediately. "No, I have to get him back to Boston, all his records are there. He is a cardiac patient," I said. "If you take him back to Boston without doing surgery, Mrs. Cronin, you will take him in a box," the doctor replied. Startled and scared, I agreed to surgery. But I added, "You're not going to give me trouble about saving his life, are you?" He said, "No, we don't say that here."

I tried calling Jim, who had taken the day off and was playing golf somewhere. A friend went to every golf course and finally found him.

Jimmy got through this surgery, but the doctor came to me and said, "We have another problem. Jimmy's been exposed to chickenpox. The baby in the next incubator came down with it. This could be really, really serious." I was drained. He went on, "There is an antibody, a serum that could be sent in by helicopter from Atlanta, Georgia, but we can't let the doctors in Georgia know that it will be used on someone with Down syndrome." (Apparently, it was very dear in all senses of the word.) Because this doctor omitted that last bit of information when ordering, the serum was flown in and given to Jimmy. In a couple of days we were headed back to Boston. That was June; he was ten months old.

Back home, after his heart surgery, Jimmy was put on liquid Digitalis twice a day. The gravity of giving it to him accurately was underscored. You needed to measure a very specific dose from the bottle into the syringe; there could not be a *single* bubble in it, which would alter the dose; too much medication would put him into cardiac arrest; too little and his heart would race. It was such a burden; I was terrified. I scheduled the doses for 7 am and 7 pm, but because I was so intent on getting this perfect, I would be up at 6 am with such worry. The stress was such that if I got it right, I would just collapse at the kitchen table. Now I know there is an easier way to do this, but then I was hyper-vigilant.

Each incident added to the armor I was forming. From the minute Jimmy was born, things were adversarial. I felt that someone was trying to take him away from me or do him harm. Whenever I turned around I heard, "He isn't going to make it." My parents, too, would look at me and comment, "Didn't we tell you?" They didn't want to see me suffer, I am sure. In my eyes, even the general population did not seem to see Jimmy's worth. I could not understand this nor could I convince people. Finally, I realized that I needed all the energy I could summon to fight for Jimmy so instead of arguing, I went inward. It became a very lonesome time.

Alone

I internalized all of this and had nobody to hash things out with. My husband had withdrawn; my family, including Bob in Illinois, did not agree with my decision to keep Jimmy alive, and there were no close friends. In the beginning, our friends were great; many donated blood in Jimmy's name. Jim's workplace was also very supportive initially. People rallied around but, when his illnesses became a way of life, the support began to fall away. Other friends who we thought were close had babies, but their children didn't have these medical issues. We got old real fast. Every time someone called, they would get a "Jimmy's sick" story. I have seen this happen to others with lives that become consumed with medical emergencies. People really do not want to hear. It is an extremely isolated existence.

Jimmy's serious emergencies meant that the trauma was affecting me. I was not able to separate an earache from heart failure. I became too afraid to stand by and wait, always wondering where one thing would lead. Everything took on a sense of urgency, even if he got a cold. I brought Jimmy home one night, put him in his high chair and called my mom to tell her he was home. All of a sudden I heard these train noises, coming from Jimmy's chest – loud, labored breaths in, and short, breaths out. "Mom, he's not breathing right." I dropped the phone, grabbed him and my pocketbook and raced to the hospital. He was having a major croup attack; I did not even know what that was at the time. He was put in an oxygen tent and given prednisone. I eventually took him home, but at night you would hear his cough, which sounded like a seal barking. I would wake in a second, get him into the bathroom and run the shower for steam until I ran out of hot water. I also ran vaporizers so often in both the bathroom and his bedroom that the wallpaper peeled right off the walls.

From the beginning, I was determined to put Jimmy's needs first and figure out what I could do to respond to those needs. My husband, however, responded with anger and, slowly but surely, what was bubbling erupted and penetrated deep into our relationship. I would try to bring him into the fold, but he did not want it. He was angry that he did not get the son he wanted, angry that my attentions were not on him, angry that we did not have our friends anymore, and angry that the focus of our life was not on having fun. Both our Disney scripts ended; he withdrew from Jimmy and me and coped with his anger in ways that were not helpful. The blaming began.

My father had an army blanket, which I tucked into a trunk in the basement of our raised ranch. When I was home alone there was no reason to go into a closet, but that is where I would go. Inside, with the door closed, I put the army blanket over my head, sat down and cried. I did not want to be seen; I did not want to be heard, not that there was anyone else in the house to hear me. I gushed with a deep, profound sobbing. I could not share it with the empty air; I could not share it with the daylight. I was desolate.

Life Begins and Expands

A shimmer of hope came, as it always does. My cousin, Dr. Jim, had always been a bit of a hero to me. At that time, he began phoning every week from Indiana. He would process the medical information I gave him, explain it in a way I could understand, and encourage me. I would say, "Jim, they want me to give up the baby." He would answer, "Well, do you want to?" "NO!" I would scream. "Then don't," he'd reply. Our conversation would continue with me asking, "Well, then what am I going to do?" "You're going to be this baby's mom," he'd say. "Well, what is he going to be like when he's 12?" I would ask. He would state, "I don't know, but let's wait and find out. If you can't handle it then, give him up at 12." I loved that because he reminded me not to create problems that I did not have yet. To this day, we still go out to see him twice a year. I guess I got what I really needed – one person calling *once* a week, faithfully. Dr. Jim, my guardian angel, held me together.

Almost a year after his birth, Jimmy was finally home to stay. However, he still had to undergo getting tubes in his ears and had to fight off numerous bad colds. On top of that, he had a blocked tear duct, which meant he had a constant weepy eye and, often, conjunctivitis. (He had that surgically corrected when he was three.) Our life, now, had an addition – a new baby brother for Jimmy named Brendan.

At 18 months old, two days before Brendan was born, Jimmy took his first step. When I brought Brendan home from the hospital, Jimmy was quite standoffish. Brendan, on the other hand, was outrageously attracted to Jimmy, loving him from the time he set eyes on him. As babies, they did everything together; they were soul mates.

Brendan often got croup, and Jimmy still seemed to get it all the time. Their breathing would wake me. I would grab them both and head quickly into the bathroom, one on one knee and one on the other, praying we would not run out of hot water. They were so pale, barely able to hold their heads up, and they were blue around their mouths from lack of oxygen. During those long nights, I was terrified.

Jim traveled often at this time, so from Sunday until Friday I was usually home alone with both boys. Jimmy was in and out of the hospital with bad ear infections, and Brendan had ten ear infections during the first 11 months of his life. I saw a lot more of my pediatrician than I did of my husband. I was constantly caring for sick kids. I did not have my mother around, and my mother-in-law was not that helpful. When Jim came home, he was tired and frustrated that things were so chaotic. I imagine it was not pleasant to come home to sick kids and an exhausted wife.

We were looking at life through two different filters.

Despite the stresses in our family and my efforts to help Jim with his resentment, I knew I had to stay focused on my two young sons. I remember bringing both boys to a neighbor's house for tea; I held Brendan in my arms while Jimmy tried to toddle around. In the middle of this outing Jimmy waddled over to me, pulled up my pant leg and bit my leg as hard as he could. Despite the pain, I was relieved – he *did* have an attachment to me. Jimmy had seen so many nurses, so many caregivers, and so many hospital beds – I did not think he had had enough time to bond with me.

Jimmy continued to prove he had ample testosterone. He loved to pull Brendan's mop of curly hair. As Brendan was learning to stand up, Jimmy would pull his hair so hard, he would pull him right back down to the ground. Furious, I would tell Brendan to pull Jimmy's hair back. At a very early age, Brendan would say, "No, I don't want to hurt him." I did everything to get Jimmy to stop tormenting Brendan; even pulling Jimmy's hair myself!

Though he could toddle, Jimmy liked his walker and was a little terror on wheels. He would crash into the dog, then get back up and do it again, just to get the dog to move. He did not seem angry, but he definitely had some aggression; he was going to take down the little brother *and* take out the dog.

Brendan did not sense anything was different about Jimmy, even when Jimmy would drool or when his conjunctivitis eye wept. I would worry, saying, "Brendan, don't be in Jimmy's face with all that." Brendan would not care; they would continue to hug and kiss. For a good long while they remained on the same cognitive level. Even when I saw Brendan pass by Jimmy, I never saw him move away emotionally. In fact, Brendan shared my awe of Jimmy. Brendan's friends eventually became Jimmy's friends. He would always say, "C'mon Jimmy, you're on my team." He would tell his buddies, "We are going to give Jimmy four strikes instead of three" – always he gave Jimmy an advantage.

I spent an inordinate amount of time with Jimmy either because he was sick or I was working intently to improve his fine and gross motor abilities. Brendan never showed any jealousy; actually, he was right there helping me. This little, three-foot-high person would eventually push Jimmy on the swing screaming, "Push your feet out." It is because of Brendan that Jimmy is a great pumper today!

Looking for Help and Finding School

I had no idea what services were out there for someone with Down syndrome, but that became my mission. I found myself in the town library searching and reading all there was on Mongoloids. Strange, quirky facts jumped out and have stuck with me ever since. For example, I read that people with Down syndrome cannot carry a tune. I also remember reading Dale Evans and Roy Rogers' book on their daughter who died from the same hole in her heart that Jimmy had. The books all seemed to focus on what they could not do. I put them down.

I learned of an agency called the ARC.* I called, and someone named Dan answered.

"Can you give me any information on Down syndrome, books or pamphlets to read, any referrals, any other people I might talk to?" I asked. He explained that this was his first day on the job and, for now, he was the executive director, the answering service, and the staff.

"Well, do you know anyone who can babysit or help me?" I asked. He thought for a second and then came back with, "Well, my girlfriend might." I pictured this young guy in a cubby of an office now volunteering his who-knows-what kind of girlfriend out back. I panicked, "Ah, no thanks, never mind."

I decided a more direct route would be to call the school system. "What is out there for my child, what's in town, what is anywhere?" I was informed that, in fact, our town had a special education director named George Mack. I called him and introduced myself. He could hear my bewilderment and actually took pity on me. Bypassing the required age of three, George started Jimmy at the Kennedy-Donovan Center – a community-based education and therapeutic program begun in 1969 in Kingston, MA. It was still new and in borrowed space. When he was just a little over two years old, Jimmy would set off two half-days each week with his lunch box in one hand and his box of pampers firmly tucked under his other arm. The Kennedy-Donovan Center gave the illusion of all play, but it was *all* therapy with extremely skilled and dedicated teachers, especially those in speech. I got involved, helping to arrange and bake for holiday parties. I don't know who I thought I was, but I even spoke to one of their parent groups about Down syndrome. Here *I* was the one looking for information. My ulterior motive in getting so immersed was to check out the kinds of activities they did so I could replicate them at home without spending a lot of money.

When we were not in Kingston, Brendan, Jimmy and I could be found zipping, buttoning, pouring and stacking for hours. We spent a lot of time, too, picking up coins with our pincer grip (thumb and forefinger). I would also hang whiffle balls from the ceiling in the basement

---

* The Arc of the United States is an organization serving people with intellectual and developmental disabilities. The organization was originally founded in the 1950s by parents of individuals with disabilities. Since that time, it has established state chapters in 39 states, with 730 local chapters in states across the country.

so they could practice hitting them with a bat. Each morning I would hang the balls from the drop ceiling using string and thumb tacks. I would make sure to take them down before Jim set foot in the house. He made it clear he didn't want holes in his ceiling.

When Jimmy turned three he went to the Kennedy-Donovan Center every day. I would get up very early to feed him and then give him a bath; I never wanted Jimmy's hair to smell like waffles. Truthfully, I never wanted anyone to think he was not clean; it would be just one more strike against him.

I loved the Kennedy-Donovan Center, but a kindergarten-type program for seven or eight special needs kids was starting in town. The special education director hired an exceptionally competent, first-year teacher and several dedicated aides. All were unmistakably professional, presenting parents with realistic expectations, clear guidelines and specific goals. I was thrilled. Students learned to sit in a circle, take turns, line up, etc. The staff loved Jimmy. As a matter of fact, one of the aides was so smitten with Jimmy that she asked to take him home and introduce him to her family. He first met her husband, Peter, and then her son, also named Peter. Seconds later, Jimmy cocked his head and questioned, "Peter, and Peter again?"

Frequently, I went in to the program to observe and noticed that Jimmy was always last in line. I told the teacher that I did not want him continuously at the end. "I don't care where he is, but I don't want him to always get his own way," I said. Jimmy had figured out that being last allowed him to stop at the water fountain for a drink! I went on, "Sometimes he can't have a drink; sometimes he can. Sometimes he has to be in the middle, and sometimes he can be the line leader." I was recalling one of those odd facts I had read back while in the library – "rigidity was a difficult and common characteristic of Mongoloids." I was determined that my kid was *not* going to be stubborn and unyielding.

Sitting and having temper tantrums also was not going to happen. The teacher and her aides worked with me on this. Jimmy did not like it, but thankfully, we broke this trait early. Jimmy is incredibly flexible and accommodating today. He will speak his mind if he does not like something, as he should, but he is not ruling the roost.

The staff was loving but tough, and so was I. My mother-in-law used to threaten that she would call social service officials on me before "human rights" was on anyone's radar. She did not like the discipline she saw me impose on Jimmy. When she visited, for example, we would sit on the couch to talk. I would tell Jimmy that he could NOT touch a particular item on the coffee table. I would show him everything else on the table that he *could* touch, but emphasized the one thing that was off limits. Naturally, when she and I resumed our conversation, Jimmy headed right for the coveted item. "What did Mommy say?" I would ask and emphasize again that he could not touch it. When he went for it a second time, he would get his hand slapped. My mother–in-law was indignant. She pointed out to me that, after all, I was fussing over a wooden object. I told her that that was not the point; I had told him "No." Jimmy learned obedience. I was resolute on this. I was not going to have behavior issues with any of my children, but especially not with my child who had special needs. The world already was not seeing Jimmy for the person he was, and I so wanted the world to welcome him.

My mother- in-law grew to love Jimmy but never in my life did she say a kind word to me. Despite trying to turn the tides, I had to accept that she just did not like me. At the end of her life, she moved in with us for a while and I took care of her. Once, getting her into the shower, she turned to me and said, "I will always be grateful to you." I thought she meant for taking care of her, but I asked anyway. "For what?" "For teaching the rest of us to love Jimmy." I did not need another compliment from this woman and never got one, but I will take that one to the bank.

Moving and A New Addition

Up to this point, the four of us were living in a small ranch. It had one bathroom the size of a phone booth. One morning I prepared to take my four-second shower, placing Jimmy on the potty seat and Brendan on a porta-potty on the floor in front of me. I gave them both books to read while I, now six months pregnant with our third child, jumped in. When my four seconds were up, I went to pull the shower curtain open and there, at the sink, was my husband shaving. The whole family was in this teensy bathroom. There was no room for me to get out and dry off. "I am going to look for a new house – today!" Jim furiously fired back, saying, "No! We can't afford it." As soon as I dried off I went to the yellow pages, looked under realtor and called one named Grace. "Grace, I need a house... now." I had no idea what company she worked for or even who she was, but that day we started looking and kept looking until I exhausted all listings within our budget. I specifically wanted a neighborhood with lots of kids and a cul-de-sac. I fell in love with a wonderful house that met all the requirements. Jim tried every which way to get out of it, even calling the realtor behind my back telling her to cancel the sale, saying, "We can't afford it." I saw his point. He wanted to cling to our current mortgage payment of $345 a month, but it just was not doable for our growing family. The stress and tension Jim felt over change gave him horrible anxiety.

I knew we could afford it, so I had our realtor sit down with us and show us again, step by step, that the numbers worked. I simply went ahead and, while very pregnant and with two little guys in diapers, I started packing boxes *and* put our house on the market. On July 4, two months before my due date, my water broke. Jim, home for the holiday, gathered the two boys and drove me to the local hospital which, in turn, sent me straight to a hospital in Boston by ambulance. Doctors told me it was a *partial* leak, but now my pregnancy was considered "high risk." I was ordered to take it easy. How do you do that with a house to pack?

I continued to do what I knew I had to do. Not long after, while vacuuming for a house showing, I suddenly felt as though I was going into labor. With Jim away, I called an ambulance who took us *all* to the hospital. I was sent home and told to be careful. It fell on my deaf ears; I had too much to do. In another few weeks, I was back in another ambulance with both little boys right next to me – thank God for my father-in-law who kept bringing us back home. With the house mostly packed up, I cleaned it beyond clean, even getting high school girls to come in and spruce it up after I finished.

Our house sold and papers needed to be signed but, on September 10, 1980, I knew this baby was coming. Jim and I zoomed off in one car to the hospital and our realtor followed. Right there, in the labor room, with Kevin minutes from being born, one page after the other was put in front of me to sign while I was stretched out on the gurney. Even as I was going into the delivery room, the realtor wanted one more signature. I thought, one day I will laugh at this, but I was not laughing then.

Ready or not, convenient or not, straight from the hospital we all moved into the new house. I couldn't find a thing and, to make matters worse, the house was filthy. I don't think the previous owner even owned a sugar bowl; if you opened the cupboards you could pull the sugar off the shelves. Pepper and other spices were everywhere. The previous owners left clothes in the closets and old toys rusting in the backyard. The bathrooms looked like they had never been cleaned. Here I was trying to toilet-train the kids and found we could not even use them.

Settling In

All three boys were in diapers; Jimmy was five, Brendan was three and Kevin was four days old. Jim still traveled Sunday through Friday. I stood at our big, bay window one evening with the baby in my arms, Brendan hanging on me like he always did, and Jimmy nearby on the couch. I watched as other fathers in the neighborhood drove into their driveways at 6 pm, looking eager to go inside. I would have tears in my eyes knowing it would be three more days before anyone pulled into my driveway to give me help. When Jim did get home, he would get frustrated by the tricycles and bikes in the driveway. I looked at the assembly of bikes and thought of the children playing happily in the backyard. Jim looked at them as obstacles, which fired his anger. Again, our vision of the same sight was so different. In hindsight, we did not take enough time to understand the other's view. I loved Jim and missed him. We were both struggling with constant demands from every direction. Instead of pulling together we were pulling apart.

The first day in our new house, four neighborhood children rang the front doorbell. Keep in mind they were little, just five, six or seven years old. The mere sight of these little kids at my front door told me that it was a perfect neighborhood for us. For one, these little guys were running around in a pack, like the *Little Rascals*, so it had to be safe, and it was welcoming. The "leader," named Craig, spoke up, asking, "Are you the new neighbors?" Two seconds later, astute and confident, he blurted out, "What's wrong with *him*?" "Who's him?" I asked. "Him," he pointed. "What's he, retarded?" I answered, "As a matter of fact he is." Without a minute's hesitation, Craig put his arm around Jimmy's shoulders saying, "That's all right buddy, you can play with us," and proceeded to lead him away. "Wait a second!" I choked. He responded, "Don't worry, I'll take care of him." Craig might have been the kingpin, but I was still staring at a five-year-old. Calmly, with a bribe up my sleeve, I said, "I think we'll not go anywhere. How about cookies in the backyard? Everyone's welcome! I'd like to get to know you guys; I wouldn't even know where to look for Jimmy if you all took off." After cookies in the back with the "posse," we were golden and our backyard became a gathering spot for playing *kick the can, hide and seek*...you name it. Jimmy was one of the gang.

Jim and His Yard

The choice of neighborhoods was looking perfect for us. To keep up appearances, Jim started on a mission to make our yard into a *Better Homes and Gardens* showcase.

Jim referred to *his* lawn as the "Augusta National" and devoted all his time at home to creating a flawless yard. He took no prisoners when people innocently walked on his lawn or even watered plants the "wrong" way. Once a young girl was helping me in the garden and watered the roses from above. Jim's reaction was so strong this poor girl got a nose bleed from the stress. All I could say was, "Doesn't God water roses from the top?"

To greet my kids when they got off the school bus, I put a pink and white checkered blanket from my childhood on the front lawn where I would be waiting with cookies and juice. All three boys would pile off the bus and land on this blanket. It was our island; our safety net. Other kids in the neighborhood eyed the cookies and wanted to sit too, but Brendan would say, "No, this is the Cronin blanket. You cannot come on it." Jimmy, Brendan and Kevin would then pull their school papers from their backpacks and we'd talk about what happened during the day. After our snack, we would dust the crumbs off ourselves and the blanket, pick up the Dixie cups and go about our afternoon. Any day the weather cooperated, that pink blanket was out. We didn't share this ritual with my husband because his rule was, "No one is allowed on my lawn."

Money was always tight but I believe that God found favor with me in this respect. Every day, I got a hold of the mail and sometimes checks would come in. For example, if we overpaid a bill, we received a reimbursement – $3, $15, even $100. I decided to open a savings account at a different bank in another town. Whenever I could save $10 here and there, I socked it away into that account. Jim gave me money for groceries, so if there was a special on meat that week I bought it and put the extra money into my account. My mother-in-law opened a similar account since Jim's father was equally tight when he doled out the weekly allowance. She called her stash her "blueberry" money. When asked what I wanted for my birthday, I would always suggest a check. Those checks, always for $20, went into my own "blueberry" fund.

Big Wheels and Big Hopes

The neighborhood kids were all on bikes and big wheels. I got a big wheel for Jimmy. Every day, for months, I got a rope and pulled the bike while teaching Jimmy right from left, "Push right, push left." Then I would run around behind him and push. He was getting it, but it was slow. One day I was out getting my mail and ended up talking with a neighbor. Out of nowhere, like a flash of lightning, Jimmy flew by on his big wheel. It *was* startling. I looked back at my neighbor with a smile on my face only to see her start to cry. When I asked if she was okay, she choked up, saying, "I have seen you working on this forever. This is such a big deal. Everyone in this neighborhood takes it for granted when our kids jump on a big wheel. You worked for this. I am jealous of you; *you* get it, you appreciate the small things!" I replied, "He worked at this too!" Jimmy went on to become a big wheel terror; he was up and down people's steep driveways, skidding and even leaving rubber.

There was a huge rock in our front yard. Once Jimmy learned to ride his big wheel, I enacted what became known as "Mrs. Cronin's Neighborhood Rule," which went like this: "Nobody goes past the rock! You can get off at the rock, you can sit on the rock, you can play on the rock, but you cannot go *beyond* the rock." This demarcation marked the distance I could see from the house and it prevented Jimmy from charging out onto a busy street. Everyone obeyed. If *any* of the kids were not in my sight, I was not happy.

We were often in the dark trying to teach Jimmy, but some of our problems were resolved when we learned he was left handed. To this day, he bats right handed but catches and throws left handed. Until his left-handed dominance became obvious, I assumed it was his disability that got in the way. I looked everywhere for a left-handed person to teach him to tie his shoes. Of all people, his very right-handed grandfather, who had no patience for anything, taught him. Jimmy survived that; I thought he would be wearing Velcro forever.

Jimmy was fitting into the neighborhood and successfully finished his second year at the remarkable elementary school program. It was structured, the teacher was organized, the staff worked as a team, therapists made constructive home visits, goals were individually crafted and meetings with parents were frequent. Teachers listened to me *and* they heard me, validating my knowledge of who Jimmy was and applauding my goals for him. I felt like I was part of the team; it was synergy in motion. Over his short time there, Jimmy made noticeable achievements socially, academically and personally.

When Jimmy turned six that next September, the special education director told me that he would go on to a six-year program at another elementary school in town. It was to be an academic and socialization program for special needs kids in town between the ages of six and 12; mainstreaming was not yet a term or a concept.

I began marinating in optimism thinking of Jimmy's move to the new school in the fall. First of all, Brendan would be there; I loved that they would see each other in the hallways. I was also thrilled that Jimmy was going to have a male teacher. Ernie had been in this teaching position for a while and I had not heard anything negative. Jimmy would have six years with him; I only envisioned him flourishing.

School Daze

Jimmy entered Ernie's program knowing his numbers and letters. He knew the sounds of letters and had a cluster of sight words you could count on. I knew Jimmy had an incredible memory, so I was sure he was going to learn to read. His fine motor skills were also good after the numerous hours spent buttoning, zipping and picking up coins. If anything needed attention, it would have been Jimmy's handwriting. He loved to answer the phone at home, often telling the person calling that I was not home. Then he would grab a piece of paper and diligently try to write down who it was who called. His notes were often illegible, so I put a typewriter on the kitchen table and began to teach him how to type. He loved the fact that this was a useful machine and was eager to conquer it. When he would come home from school, before he even talked to me about his day, I would have him type me something. Sometimes the page looked like a traffic jam of random letters but, slowly, he got the hang of it; it might have been elementary, but he began to get his point across. What possibility, I thought!

After his new school year with Ernie got underway, I happily set off to observe Jimmy in his class, just as I had done at both the Kennedy-Donovan Center and at his first elementary school. Programs for Jimmy thus far had been stellar; I was excited to see what this advanced program had in store. But, just entering Ernie's classroom gave me pause. I stood for a moment and looked around. Something was dramatically different. I saw seven or eight students, varying in age from six to 12. What was immediately apparent was that this class had every single diagnosis imaginable – from behavior issues and physical disabilities to retardation, autism and head banging. There might have been one other boy with Down syndrome.

I happened on an art project. In actuality, it was an art fiasco with glue flying (and landing) all over the table while one boy rested his curly-haired head on the table. Nobody seemed to be in charge. This went on for a bit until Ernie stopped everything for snack time. I then watched in horror as crackers were placed in front of each student on this glue-globbed table. There was no attempt to wash either the table or the students' hands despite a working sink in the room. Clearly Jimmy and all these students would have benefitted from instruction on basic hygiene skills. What a lost opportunity! Even offering a paper towel to put the crackers on would have been less disturbing.

Snack time continued to be unnerving. The students, like feral animals, grabbed for each other's food. Neither Ernie nor his aide stopped the behavior, much less discussed it. Another teachable moment overlooked – a lesson on manners missed.

Shortly after snack, on the way to lunch, one student stopped at the door to look at himself in the mirror. Appropriately, I thought, he used his hand to smooth out his messy hair. Instead of seeing this as a chance to review yet another social skill, Ernie pushed him playfully from behind saying, "Don't bother looking at yourself, nobody else is." A short hour inside this room left a marked pall on any optimism I had.

After several visits, things did not appear to be any sunnier. I continuously noticed a lack of academics in the classroom. I wondered about Jimmy's objectives. What would be the outcome of ten months in this program? Having had such a clear understanding of Jimmy's goals from his other program, I asked Ernie for an education plan.* What I got was a sneer and a disparaging reply: "I don't *do* ed plans."

*Education plans were mandated in 1975 when the United States Congress passed the Education for All Handicapped Children Act. The EHA was later modified to strengthen protections to people with disabilities and renamed the Individuals with Disabilities Education Act (IDEA). The school is required to develop and implement an IEP that meets the standards of federal and state educational agencies.

"No ed plan?" I asked incredulously. "How do you keep track of goals?" He pointed to his head, "They're all up here." I told him that I found that absolutely frightening. "What happens if you get hit by a bus? Whoever takes over needs to know what Jimmy can do and where he is going." Ernie simply shook his head impertinently and walked away.

Confused, I went to the special education director and asked why there was no ed plan. His response? "It takes a while to get used to a new program, Connie." At home, my husband was also clashing with me, harping that I should not cause problems.

This was all too odd for me; things did not sit well. Each time I went to the school my eyes opened wider, my gut would knot and my mind jumped to conclusions, conclusions I didn't want to be making. I continued to visit, hoping to be encouraged by something, anything. But that "something" never came; instead, old but vivid images of dismal, dirty institutionalized settings haunted me every time I entered Ernie's room.

Despite being terribly bothered I had a greater and ever-growing concern. By mid-year, Jimmy was beginning to show speech difficulties. I wondered if it could be brought on by emotional issues. I had read that spinning stimulates language and even saw that Jimmy would dance in a spin here and there, but the staff at school always stopped it. I started taking Jimmy to playgrounds; I would put him on swings and twist the chains tightly, purposely, so they would unravel in lickety-split speed. Right after those outings his speech improved. I then begged Jim to put a swing up for Jimmy. Jim didn't want to, saying a swing would damage his lawn, but I prevailed in getting one placed in a far corner. Jimmy would go outside and blissfully swing forever. I don't think the small improvements in his speech were a coincidence; I think he was getting that vestibular stimulus.

Along with asking Jim for the swing, I asked Ernie to have his program's speech and language therapist evaluate Jimmy. My simple request was soon to unearth illuminating information about the program's lack of services. Speech therapy, he told me, was not a regularly scheduled occurrence, nor was occupational or physical therapy. Ernie had the use of the one therapist who serviced *all* the students in the school, so an evaluation for Jimmy would take time, if it happened at all. Looking around at the severity of needs in Jimmy's classroom, I didn't think this was good programing but, at that point, I did not know what I did not know; I had no other program model to compare it to. The puzzle, however, was beginning to take form: no scheduled therapies meant no paper trail, and no ed plans meant no paper trail. This meant there was no accountability on Ernie's part, or the school's.

I persisted in making it known that I wanted an evaluation; Jimmy's speech was disintegrating and I did not want it to decline any further. He had gone into Ernie's program fluent and intelligible, now his communication was problematic and worrisome; he started to hesitate and show blocking and stuttering issues. I asked again, but the special education director said the town did not want to pay for an outside evaluation. I soon decided I did not want to wait, so I took Jimmy to Boston for a thorough speech evaluation, including a brain scan. When Jim would ask me how I was paying for this, I told him I had my ways. That blueberry money was coming in handy.

I didn't know what to expect, but I began hoping that the neurologist would find that he was having seizures. At least that would mean medication might resolve his dsyfluency. Instead, I learned that he now had Verbal Apraxia, a motor speech disorder in which the brain has difficulty coordinating muscle movements. I was told he needed intensive speech therapy, three to five times a week, and quickly.

My hands seemed tied. How would I get this for Jimmy? I tried to set up a meeting with Ernie, the special education director, his teacher and whatever therapists were part of Jimmy's life. Nothing came of my request, just more discouraging and confusing news. Ernie told me that in his program there were no parent meetings. Summer was now upon us; I had a lot to mull over.

My Other Life – My Family

All through these taxing years in Ernie's classroom, I had another full-time job at home trying to manage the health issues of my other children. Kevin had severe allergies and, at age three, he was diagnosed with classic asthma. For the next ten or so years, Kevin suffered terribly and many days were terrifying. Because my husband traveled all week, I was forever calling neighbors in the middle of the night to ask them to come stay with Jimmy and Brendan while I drove Kevin, unable to breathe, to the hospital.

Along with the asthma there were skin issues. Kevin's crib sheets would be so bloodied in the morning from a terrible, itchy rash all over his body. His allergist told me to soak him in a bath with Domeboro – packets of astringent powder. He couldn't stay in the bath long enough, so I devised a way to wrap him like a mummy in soaked strips of gauze while he lay having a snack and watching TV. It was not until adolescence that his asthma and the eczema condition abated.

Kevin's well-being was a constant worry, but Brendan, too, was sick off and on in these years. There were plenty of other ambulances called for various "growing-up" injuries, one caused from falling from a tire swing, resulting in a severe concussion. There were broken bones, stitches, swollen black eyes from missed baseballs – all typical "boy" misfortunes that seemed to be regular occurrences in my family.

My time researching what to do about Jimmy's schooling was important, but I was also stretched to the near max at home.

Cub Scouts and that Community Feeling

Anywhere you spotted a seven-year-old boy, Cub Scouts was the talk, especially at school and on the bus. That summer all the neighborhood boys were planning on joining. Jimmy was now of age and he was so eager to belong. I took him to sign up on that designated August day. An official looking woman, dressed in an impeccable scout uniform with her kerchief properly knotted at the neck, handed me the form. I filled it out while Jimmy ran around with his friends and then handed it back to her saying, "Perhaps you would like to meet your new Cub Scout." "No, it isn't necessary," she replied dismissively. "Well," I went on, "It might be in this case. You might want to assign him to a smaller troop or just think a little about what den mother might be the best fit." She went on shuffling her papers without answering, so I snagged Jimmy, brought him over and began the introductions.

"This is my son, Jimmy Cronin, and *he's* going to be a new Cub Scout." Jimmy said gleefully, "Yea!" She took one look at him, shook her head and hastily said, "Oh, no he's not!" Without a moment's hesitation, right in front of us, she took our application in both hands and proceeded to rip it in half, from top to bottom and then threw it in the trash can. I can see it vividly, even today. For a moment I was numb, aware only of all the kids running around. But there was Jimmy next to me, poking me, saying incredulously, "I am going to be a Cub Scout, right?" You could have taken a buzz saw right then and there and cut me in half. That was the most painful experience I have lived through to date. I did not want to cry in front of Jimmy, but I sensed tears blurring my eyes and felt the heat of my anger rising.

Jim came home that night and asked me what was going on. The incident was still raw, but I went through the story, blow by crushing blow. Jim said nothing, which startled me at first, but then I realized that this scout master's reaction resonated with him. He, like her, thought I was pushing the limits with Jimmy. His answer to this, however, was to call a colleague of his in a nearby town who was involved in the scouts. I took the phone and this acquaintance said that there was a Cub Scout troop at Cardinal Cushing.

I interrupted. "I don't want him in a scout troop over at Cardinal Cushing; he doesn't *go* to Cardinal Cushing. I want him with his friends. That is where he goes to school, where he knows kids, and where he lives. And when he sees kids in the hallway wearing their Cub Scout uniform, I want *that* to be a bonding thing." He paused but went on. "Well, if you can't get a scout troop in Hanover, I will take him in Whitman." I was not getting my point across. "I don't want him shipped off to another town or to a special needs group where he doesn't know anyone. It doesn't make any sense. He needs to be with his peers. I want him to have friends nearby."

Jim's acquaintance finally heard me and soon afterwards called someone in the national program, the Boy Scouts of America. That big wig called the little wig in town who, in turn, was pressured into calling different den mothers. She phoned one den mother by the name of Carol and said, "There's a pushy mother in town trying to shove her special needs kid into a place he doesn't belong, which is *our* Cub Scouts. Until she goes away we must find a troop for him. I don't know if you'd take this kid." Carol asked the scout leader, "Are you talking about Connie Cronin?" (Little did this "leader" realize that Carol knew of me – her son and my Brendan went to school together.) Carol called immediately, regaling me with the whole story, word for word, ending with the favorable news that she would happily take Jimmy in her troop.

It was at this point that my husband began accusing me of creating problems. I did realize that people were becoming aware that I was looking out for Jimmy's best interest, but I was not taking anyone else's best interest away; I just wanted Jimmy to be part of the community.

Carol made Jimmy feel so welcome; the kids loved him, and I still get Christmas cards from the assistant den leader telling me how Jimmy changed her life. He was in Cub Scouts for as long as you can be a Cub Scout. Then, in fourth grade, he went on to the Webelos, a 20-month transition experience leading to Boy Scouts. His leader was, of all people, the husband of the woman who ripped up our application.

At one point in this experience, fathers were asked to go on a camping trip. It was a great experience for Jim and Jimmy. Jim was surprised to learn what Jimmy could do. At home, he might have been amazed at seeing Jimmy succeed once in raking leaves correctly, but he didn't think it could happen again. Any success of Jimmy's was, to Jim, an isolated incident and he did not see that working at something would improve it. Like many parents, I later learned, Jim thought "this is as good as it gets, and it's good enough for what I got."

Graduating from the Webelos entailed a tradition of crossing a bridge to a special campfire, where a culminating speech was given by the den leader. When Jimmy graduated, his den leader began, "I would like to mention a special scout who has completely changed my life and the life of all these scouts. Years ago, kids like this were kept in closets; they were hidden away and not included. But this boy's mother insisted that he should be a scout and it has changed the scouting experience for every one of us here." This man's wife was at the campfire but acted as if nothing had ever happened between us.

With the Webelos over, Jimmy tried four Boy Scouts meetings. I tagged along to several of them, sat in the back, and saw firsthand that this grouping was very different – pre-adolescent boys running in packs. They were so physical, even rough with each other. Not one of them acknowledged Jimmy. The gap was beginning and Jimmy felt it. We did not pursue Boy Scouts.

Everything happening in Jimmy's life – his lousy programing, his poor health, his deteriorating speech – was superimposed over the stresses of our other life, the so-called *normal* life, a life with three children, a traveling husband and no family nearby to help. It was not a bad life, but it was incredibly hectic. Add to that the people I ran into regularly: people with negative attitudes, people with prejudices ("he doesn't belong"), people who simply wouldn't "play" right. I got so tired of trying to convince people that there was value here.

Those who said Jimmy did not belong because "it hasn't been done before" made me cringe. But maybe I had the reverse prejudice – thinking that Jimmy belonged everywhere.

Tackling Jimmy's Elementary Education

It was back to school in the fall after stewing all summer about Jimmy's school situation. I thought about the disheartening classroom visits and tried to absorb the discouraging pieces of information I had learned as the school year ended in June. The harsh reality inside Ernie's classroom became unambiguous: this program was a charade and my poor son was in the middle of it. The scrambled pieces of the puzzle were beginning to fit snugly. For starters, Ernie didn't acknowledge or appreciate the myriad of disabilities sitting right in front of him and, clearly, there was no attention given to individual needs. There was no routine and no structure; the program was cannon-loose and scarily unpredictable. There were heaps of wasted, idle time and there was no teamwork between Ernie and his aide; he did his thing and she did hers. What's more, I never saw any student getting help with reading, writing, or math, much less with time and money skills. Social skills were not addressed, and therapies were catch as catch can. The important extras – music, art, gym, field trips, classroom themes, holiday discussions – were non-existent. Instead, school days were filled with mindless, non-educational games. To this day, Jimmy hates *Duck, Duck, Goose*.

A little information is dangerous – and that's all I had. The idea of no goals, no ed plans and no consistent therapies only stirred up more questions, which started me down a path that became rockier and rockier. I would stumble along this path for the next five *long* years. (At the end of his six years with Ernie, Jimmy could not tell time or identify money and – worse – he did not count, read or write. Our typewriter sat unused on the kitchen table.)

Just after Jimmy began his second year in Ernie's program, the neighborhood kids asked me why Jimmy was riding on the van instead of on *their* school bus. It never dawned on me, but after I thought about it I petitioned the special education director to let Jimmy ride the bus that his friends took, telling him that it picked everyone up at the end of our street and "after all, they're getting dropped at the same school." George saw no problem with this and by October had assigned him to the route. All September, the anticipation of riding the big yellow bus mounted.

On Jimmy's first day, the kids and all the neighborhood parents walked to the bus stop with cameras to mark the occasion. The bus pulled up, the driver opened the door and looked quizzically at Jimmy. Excitedly, I piped up, "Meet your new student." Horror-struck, the driver bellowed, "Not on my bus!" I felt the blood rush to my face. "Yes, on your bus," I countered with daggers. "Nobody told *me* about this," she insisted. "Nobody has an obligation to tell you; he is *going* on this bus." Defeated, she said, "Get in the back." The other kids rallied 'round. "C'mon Jimmy, come with us." After he climbed in, I said firmly, "He's a student of yours now – a passenger – just like everybody else."

What should have been a magnificent and memorable morning melted in front of me; I walked home crying every step of the way. Once inside my door and finally a bit more composed, I called George who assured me he would get to the bottom of this. He ended up telling the bus driver that Jimmy was *his* student and that "the new pick-up location for everyone would be in front of the Cronin house."

The rides to and from school seemed to be going smoothly for Jimmy, but after a month or so I decided to check in with the principal, a crotchety old man known to strike fear in the hearts of his kids and their parents. "Mr. Sargent, I am just calling to see how the bus situation is going," I said. "What are you asking?" he answered snidely. "I am wondering if there are any issues. I can't fix what I don't know, and I *do* know that Jimmy can be stubborn. So, I am calling to see if there is anything I can help you with to make this work as smoothly as possible." He answered, "You just want your kid to be normal. I have never had a phone call from a regular kid's parent asking about the bus ride." I replied from somewhere deep inside me, "Well, it may surprise you to know that I do *not* want my son to be normal. I want him to have normal experiences within the realm of his capabilities. Riding the bus is a normal experience, so if you have problems with Jimmy on that bus, you handle it." "Don't worry, I will," he boasted with a condescending air.

Wasn't it a day or two later that the bus pulled up to the house without Jimmy. I was frantic, asking the other kids as they were getting out, "Where's Jimmy?" knowing full well they were all too young and preoccupied to have noticed.

I immediately called the principal. "My son is not on the bus, what are you going to do?" "I will have to call the authorities," he answered arrogantly. I told him that I had already called the police and insisted they stop *every* yellow school bus from this elementary school. "So, your buses will be held up," I added. "You might have other parents wondering where their son or daughter is." To this day, I have never heard back from him. What did happen was that Jimmy was not being watched and got on another bus with a friend from Cub Scouts. I finally got a call from this friend's mother who said, "Jimmy's here. They're playing, he's great. Can he stay?"

Jimmy learned to manage the bus but my worries about his programming mounted. I went back to Ernie's classroom to see if there were any changes. I pleaded again, not only for a time to talk to Ernie but also for a written ed plan. Gruffly, Ernie informed me that there would be no meetings to discuss student goals, no parent consultations, and no progress reports from him, his aide or the school therapists. Period. End of conversation.

How could this program and these anomalies keep unfolding? Key pieces of this puzzle were still missing. I knew Ernie had been at this job for a while but wondered why I had not heard any negative comments from any other parent. Were they satisfied? I knew there had to be program guidelines somewhere: mandates, rules and regulations – something on a state or federal level to follow. So I went to George to ask for clarity, still hoping to learn something I had not considered. When I asked him about Ernie's dismissal of ed plans and parent meetings, the final, perhaps most colorful piece of this puzzle was handed to me. "Ernie is not a certified special ed teacher," George said. "He's been grandfathered in." As a knee-jerk reaction, in utter disbelief, I said bluntly, "Well, he can't teach Jimmy, he's not qualified." As shocking as this revelation was, the pieces of the puzzle now had a border to fit. I insisted right then and there that Ernie be removed.

George's face was cold and unflinching. He had a program that just ticked along, protected because of the supposed grandfather clause – and it was cheap. This was one class he did not have to think about. My demand for Ernie's resignation was not up for negotiation. George made it abundantly clear in this conversation, and many more to come, that I was the only one to find fault here.

I did not know how a special needs class was put together; I did not know anyone in a similar age program and I had no idea if I had legal rights – but I knew this was duplicitous. I asked everyone I could think of for information on where to go for help. I learned that I could hire a parent advocate, but soon found out I could not afford one. I finally landed at the doors of the Federation for Children with Special

Needs, which provided me with both an advocate and a legal manual. I was now locked and loaded, about to get educated. I even began advocacy training through the Federation so I could speak for myself and eventually become a support for others. The advocate assigned to me was formidable. A large woman with a commanding presence, she came with me into Jimmy's classroom a few times to observe. She confirmed my perceptions. I then insisted on reassembling those involved in Jimmy's education to meet with me and my advocate. At this point, with a little more knowledge from the Federation's manual, I honestly went to the meeting thinking that *I* was educating *them*. I was not adversarial but brought legal references to the table, trying to be informative about what to do and how to do it. I pointed out that, per public law PL94-142*, I should have a formal ed plan. Not much was said at the end of the meeting, but I left thinking, naively, "Now they get it!"

No ed plan came forward the second year. By the third year, I might have gotten a few sentences from Ernie about what he would do with Jimmy over the next month or so, but it became evident that the town was not complying. I went ahead and, from my "blueberry" money, hired an attorney. The special education director did not like this and things now began to get confrontational. A disgruntled George telephoned. "I don't know where you think you are going with this. You can get all the attorneys you want, but I have lawyers at my disposal *and* I have more money than you do, so I'll outlast you. You can't compete with me!" "That is not my intention," I started politely. "My intention is to come together with you and work for Jimmy's benefit, but if I have to buck the system, I will."

That evening, Jim phoned from out of town. I told him what had transpired with George and naively expected to hear a husband's support. Instead, Jim gave it to me with both barrels. "This has gone too far. You cannot *fight* the system; you cannot *change* the system. The school system has been in existence long before Jimmy Cronin came along, long before Connie Cronin came along. Nobody else is complaining, have you noticed? It's only *you*; something is really *wrong* with you; people think you are crazy."

*PL 94-142 Education for Handicap Children made law in 1975 and renamed IDEA (Individuals with Disabilities Education Act) in 1990 mandated, among other things, individual education plans for all special needs students.

When there was half a minute of silence, I landed on my feet. "If you are going to blow smoke in my face then get out of my way, 'cuz I am not stopping."

The events that followed didn't help matters and only strengthened my husband's new platform. I had numerous concerns about Jimmy's education and with advice from my advocate and lawyer, I began to go into Ernie's classroom two or three times a week to observe. That went on for a while until one day I was met at the entrance by a scowling, assistant vice-principal, He was standing with his arms stretched out across the double doors telling me that I was officially barred from the building. It was so disconcerting; it felt like something out of the Civil Rights movement. I told him that I was a parent with two children in his building; I could not be barred from a public school. He went on to tell me that I would no longer have free access to this school or to Ernie's classroom. Further, I could not come into the building without his permission, without Ernie's permission and without another staff member present. He concluded by telling me that this school would *not* be ready at a moment's notice to accommodate me; I needed to make an appointment if I wanted to come inside.

I was unhinged. So irritated, so humiliated, and so stuck, I had no alternative but to turn away. Frustrated, I told him that I would be back to picket with a sign that would read: "I am a parent of a special needs child in this school and I am barred from here because I care." He told me to go ahead and do whatever I wanted to, but I was *not* coming in. I seethed. This was wrong. I had not been disruptive. I had not tried to take control; I sat on a stool, in the corner, not saying a word. I simply observed and reported what I saw to the Federation of Children with Special Needs and to George. When I got home I called the Federation, which confirmed that the school's action that morning was illegal.

By now, Jimmy was nine. My meager funds to pay the lawyer were drying up and my request for an ed plan was simply a classic broken record. I was baffled that other parents in Jimmy's program either seemed to accept this or were oblivious. I decided to try and form a parents group to see what we could do to change it. I noticed a mother of one of Jimmy's classmates in her car one day and walked over and knocked on her window. "Donna, do you know that your son is in this classroom where nothing constructive is happening? I need help. Let's form a parents group." In the middle of my last sentence, she quickly rolled up her window, saying, "You're rocking the boat." Her reaction made me realize that gossip had been unleashed and was now wide-spread; this was not just between me, George and Ernie anymore. I was left to wonder if there was any truth behind my husband's fierce and persistent "you're crazy" battle cry.

One evening, Jim's father was taken to the emergency room where Jim met him. Coincidently, the chairman of the town's board of education, Mike, was there too and approached Jim, asking if he was my husband. With a "yes" from Jim, Mike proceeded with his own angry tirade. "Everyone thinks your wife is way out of line, and she is! She is going to get less for your son rather than more if she keeps causing so much trouble. She is pushing where she shouldn't be." Jim was embarrassed and angry at my attempts to bring change to the special education system. (Interestingly enough, Mike and I eventually turned out to be good friends. He came full circle and became a loyal supporter of children with special needs. I respect him greatly, but to this day, I have never asked what was being said about me.)

As much as I wanted the parents in Ernie's program to come together, it was not happening. I kept moving, however, and joined a mothers' group that was being formed through one of the ARCs. It was a large group, drawing from several adjoining towns on the South Shore. I was the *only* one from Jimmy's class for the entire six years. We met once a month, rain or shine. I was a sponge. I learned that no other program in the area resembled Jimmy's: all the others had formal IEPs (Individual Education Plans), scheduled team meetings with parents, oodles of therapy, and varied educational activities. Their children were blooming, it seemed, and when one started to plateau the classroom teacher provided new, appropriate and timely interventions.

What's more, each of their children were in a 12-month program; Jimmy's was ten months, with summers off. Mothers in this support group were aghast hearing all that was wrong and encouraged me to continue pressing for a certified teacher, an ed plan, consistent and frequent individualized speech therapy sessions, and a 12-month program. I had already witnessed Jimmy's speech regressing in Ernie's class, and he was losing what little academics he had gained. Each summer he fell even further behind in all areas. Now apprised of what was available in other programs, I realized I had to get my priorities straight and figure out what I was trying to accomplish. I did not want to be fighting, I was simply looking for a way to meet Jimmy's needs. So, despite the push backs and the demands in my own family, I could not let up.

71

Around this time, I became aware of yet another missing component in Jimmy's program. From my support group, I learned that other programs were not only participants in Special Olympics but they had coaches to prepare them, banners to carry in the opening procession, and soup-to-nuts uniforms supplied by their schools. In fact, just before the official day of the spring Special Olympics, the athletes in these other programs would parade, in full regalia, all around the school carrying their banner and relishing the enthusiasm of students lining the hallways clapping and cheering them on. There was never any talk of Special Olympics in Ernie's class, so I asked Rita, an old babysitter of Jimmy's who was studying to become a special ed teacher, if she would coach these kids. She and I, and one or two of her swarm of brothers, would be at the school yard on Saturday mornings to help shape a team for Jimmy and his classmates. (Rita coached this team throughout their elementary school years.)

We were ready to compete by spring. We had trained, filled out all the necessary forms, gotten the schedule for each event and arrived all geared up, albeit a bit rag tag. When I saw all the other athletes marching in snappy uniforms, I decided we needed to be more official looking. The following year I fundraised to buy them uniforms. Jimmy was good at the softball throw, long jump, 50-yard dash and shot put, and loved standing on the cubes to get his medals. What he didn't excel at was waiting between events; it was the first time I heard him use the word "boring." He was actually annoyed that he had to wait.

Back in the classroom, as hard as I pushed, Jimmy's speech therapy was still erratic. It seemed I was not making progress on any front. Ernie remained in the classroom, there was still no IEP, still no meetings, and Jimmy continued in a ten-month program. Summers were becoming more and more painful as Jimmy's speech and memory declined further. At one point, I honestly thought I was losing him.

Somehow, I got wind that other students in town had summer programs, so I petitioned George. I waited, but he offered no summer program for Jimmy. I quickly knew this was his way of punishing me for pushing against the system. When I would tell him that Jimmy was backsliding over the two-month break, he told me that I had to prove it. Again using my "blueberry" money, I hired independent evaluators to test Jimmy at the end of the school year in June and then again in early September. The evaluations clearly showed that there was regression in fine motor, speech, social skills, etc. It was heartbreaking, especially since he had made such a good start at the Kennedy-Donovan Center and in his elementary school program. I took the test results to George, only to hear, "Well, next year, we'll have *my* staff do the evaluations." That meant another summer wasted at home. I pleaded, "I don't want to have to keep Jimmy home to have him regress, just to prove to you what *I* already know and what these evaluations clearly show." George's answer? "If you stopped pushing, Jimmy would get more. Why do you have to make things better for everyone? You should just be concentrating on Jimmy." He must have been referring to my continuous, no-bones demands for Ernie's removal. Ernie knew that I wanted him out. I even said to him, "I don't dislike you, Ernie, and Jimmy doesn't dislike you. You're a nice man, but you are not qualified to teach my son."

I had to play George's game. His team did the next round of summer and fall evaluations. The speech and occupational therapists who did the testing called me, saying they found significant regression and had submitted the handwritten evaluation to George. A short time later they called again, saying, "We are calling to tell you that George ordered us to destroy our evaluation. We're sorry, Mrs. Cronin, it's either our job or this report." I begged them, saying, "Please stand up for Jimmy." But these young women were too scared. The evaluations were suppressed.

I knew – and now had proof – that Jimmy and his classmates were not getting the education they deserved, but no matter how I tried, I could not get a group of local special ed parents together. I didn't learn why until years later. Most didn't think they could make a difference – they actually didn't know they had any rights. Others just accepted what was in front of them, thinking that this was their lot in life. Still others didn't think their child could really *do* any more. Nearly all were just happy to have a place for their child to go every day.

I had learned from my ARC support group that if you were on the good side of the town's special education director you had a chance of getting your child into a better program. Left with no support, I asked George to put Jimmy in one of the collaborative programs. "Sure," he said, "if *you* pay for it." I then asked, "What about Cardinal Cushing right here in town?" He told me the same thing. Clearly, I was not on George's good side; he wanted me to disappear.

In Jimmy's fifth year, Ernie and George did finally produce what they said was an ed plan and they called the team together to go over it. In preparation for this meeting, I sorted through all I knew about what other programs offered, but decided I had to get my priorities for Jimmy's well-being in order. I went with only one hope. The ed plan they presented looked nothing like an official one, but there were some ideas written down. The goals, however, were neither measurable nor attainable; there was no explanation of how to achieve them, and they were not individualized for Jimmy. I said nothing as they went through the plan. Instead, the entire time I sat praying for the one thing I thought might make a difference for Jimmy – a summer program. I could not stand by and watch another two-month lapse in school happen.

When all was said and done, Ernie got up to leave. I slowly stood. George did too, but as he began to rise, he hesitated and then added, "Oh, and let's make this a 12-month program for Jimmy." The floodgates opened – I burst. I sat back down at the table and just sobbed. I was so relieved and…so broken. I do not know why George changed his mind, but I suspect it was about those "missing" therapy reports from his staff. I had gone to George and told him I knew he squelched Jimmy's evaluations. "I can't prove it because you *are* more powerful, George, and you're much richer than I am, but don't ever forget I know what the reports said, and I know they existed."

Shortly after this meeting, Ernie came up to me. "I am losing the job I love. Are you happy?" I replied, "If you *really* loved the students, Ernie, you would want them to be taught by someone who knows how to do it." I asked what he was going to do. He said he was being transferred to the high school to coach high school football and, unabashedly, added, "I'm also going to teach high school students with special needs."

I called George the minute I got home, telling him, sternly, that under *no* condition – even hell freezing over – would Jimmy ever have Ernie again. "He will *not* go through high school with him and shame on you for taking this long to move him!"

That next fall, Jimmy's final year in the program, Ernie moved to the high school. Jimmy's class opened with a brand new teacher. Within the first two months, Ernie's replacement had a nervous breakdown and had to leave. This poor neophyte came into this discombobulated program without any guidance, support or written plans for the

74

class and without any teaching experience or knowledge of how to work in a team. Jimmy's last year became more chaotic than ever. All the special education director did for the rest of the year was hire a multitude of substitute teachers who simply babysat. I now could not think of anything but getting him out of this school.

(We finally did get a decent teacher for that program. Parents who came through it later thanked me for making things better for them; but inside I suffered, knowing I had not made things better in time for Jimmy.)

Middle School and Calmer Shores

I was introduced to Jimmy's potential middle school placement at a meeting with George and the North River Collaborative's director, Dr. Patricia Maley. The Collaborative was newly opened to students with special needs from our town, but I did not know much about the operation. This initial meeting with Pat and subsequent meetings with middle school Collaborative teachers, Laura and Mary, was like the dawning of the sun. After six years of dealing with incompetency and Jimmy's decline, I was now meeting with savvy professionals who knew how to run a structured classroom creatively. Happily, I learned that there were real IEPs; scheduled, weekly therapies by a Collaborative *team* of therapists; routine team meetings with parental input; and quarterly progress reports. That was just for starters. In the end, the North River Collaborative rescued Jimmy from drowning and brought me to calmer shores.

I was, however, nervous about how the other middle school students would treat Jimmy. I decided to meet with the vice principal, Walter Sweeney, telling him that I wanted to see if this school was going to be "appropriate for my son." Walter had assumed this placement for Jimmy was etched in stone, but I did not. When we met, I asked him what he could do for Jimmy. "How can you make this school work for him? How can you protect him?" He assured me by saying that, if he had to, he would walk the halls with Jimmy's class to make sure everything was okay. Each time we met after this initial conversation, Mr. Sweeney would hug me and call me "the little spitfire." He would say, "I love this woman like a sister. She sat across from me and demanded that I prove I could educate her son. Here, I have this pilot program coming in from the North River Collaborative and now I have this 'pilot' parent."

Mr. Sweeney allayed most fears, but I had recently heard about a scary and dangerous incident on the middle school bus. I remembered too, that Jimmy had been hit on the bus and another student had come to his aid. I knew I could not rely on kids coming to Jimmy's rescue because kids' attitudes at this age towards people like my Jimmy were shifting. I decided I did not want Jimmy on the regular school bus and requested he be put on the smaller special needs van.

Soon after he switched, a couple of the neighborhood kids – provoking a feeling of déjà vu – showed up at my door asking why Jimmy was not on the bus with them. I told them that I thought middle school could be a tough time and that they had their own friends, new activities and enough to worry about. Disconcerted, with obvious sadness on their faces, they said, "Do you think we'd let anything happen to Jimmy?" I said, "No, but I don't want you to feel you have to be responsible for him either." They stood there – a little taller, a little braver and much more competent than seven years earlier – and said, "Mrs. Cronin, please, we promise *nothing* will happen to Jimmy if you put him back on the bus." I love those kids. Because of them, Jimmy rode their bus, happily and safely, for the next two years.

Life in middle school started to even out; there was a rhythm and flow that was saner. I didn't feel like I had to be on top of any of the Collaborative teachers. Jimmy was learning again; he was happier and beginning to regain his sense of self. He went on field trips, participated in the Collaborative Special Olympics, and started to learn basic vocational skills.

I even found that I had some time on my hands. One discussion that came up in my mothers' support group focused on the changing attitudes of kids towards the disabled. I felt a real tug to soften this outlook and educate the regular population as to what was really going on inside *that* classroom in their school. On public radio, coincidently, I had just heard about a kit called, *What If I Couldn't*, available at the Children's Museum in Boston. In it were ideas and props to educate school children about living with disabilities. I suggested to the group that I petition the school system to purchase it, and all the mothers rallied around the idea. I applied for the money but was denied. I applied again the following year and was granted the $500 to start a program that I called "Handicap Awareness." The kit focused on six disabilities and we embellished it as we went along. I was to do the mental retardation piece. Other mothers, despite all of us having only cognitively impaired children, took on other disabilities, such as the physical, emotional and behavioral, as well as blindness and deafness. This group of women was impressive and very committed to this cause.

Since I wanted to start with second, third and fourth graders, I had to go back to the vice principal who blatantly barred me from Jimmy's school to tell him I wanted to do something positive at his school with a team of parent volunteers. "It would educate and help the teachers as well as the students, and it would be a plus for your school," I said. With his permission, we began. The program met with success and expanded so quickly that we began to ask outside speakers, people with all different disabilities, to come and address classes.

In my presentation, I tried to make understanding mental retardation interactive so, for example, I had kids zipper coats with gloves on their hands and speak with marshmallows in their mouths. It was energizing to see the reaction of students and their teachers, and it was both stimulating and startling to hear their questions after each session. One girl asked, "Does Jimmy wash his hands?"

We were so taken aback by the questions that we decided to scale back the presentations and simply emphasize the basics – feelings. Elementary school age children do not understand that people share similar feelings. To change behaviors, we realized, these young students had to see that hurtful comments hurt no matter who they are directed at, and that embarrassing anyone stings, no matter who you are. We knew we were making a difference when kids began to confess that they had made fun of someone. The changes in attitudes became palpable; the demand for our program grew, mushrooming into a part-time job. It also mushroomed in expense. I needed to figure out how to pay for the speakers and materials we needed. I asked Dr. Maley at the North River Collaborative to help me write a grant through the Department of Education. I was brand new at this and the thought of going up in front of the Board of Education was daunting. Pat urged me on, working with me tirelessly. Because of her help, we received enough money to last for two or three years. I was told that I was the only parent who ever wrote and received a grant from the Department.

We would probably still be doing this program today, except that a teacher who was working her way up the ladder to school superintendent eyed this program and decided *she* would write a grant to pay herself and take the project over. It was going to be *her* program, run with the same parents, or so she thought. We were so insulted that we turned our backs and left. After all, we were the ones who had developed the concept, taught ourselves the material for all the disabilities, fine-tuned each presentation, and made the program a success – all, of course, without pay. She was awarded the grant money, which became her second salary, and began her program, which only lasted a year or two before dissolving.

Moving Into High School

After two years in the middle school, it was time to look at high school programs. Jimmy was put into a program, but I was not pleased; I wanted him in the Collaborative's vocational program but Anne, the teacher who ran the program, said "Let's wait a year." Luckily, I was able to convince her to take a gamble on Jimmy. Following is her perspective on having Jimmy join her classroom:

<u>My Perspective as Jimmy's Teacher:</u>

"Having run a vocational, academic and socialization program for adolescents with developmental delays for fifteen years when Jimmy arrived, I thought I had a certain understanding of the spectrum of skills one needed to be successful in the workplace. These understandings were based on three things: standardized tests, informal vocational assessments, and years of experience placing relatively high functioning people in community worksites.

"I had never worked with Jimmy; I knew him only through middle school reports and a few visits to his classroom. I wondered about his level of communication, as he presented with a pronounced stutter making him difficult to understand. His processing, too, seemed to be terribly delayed as did his ability to follow more than one-step directions. I noted that certain academic skills, in particular his ability to count, read, and work with money, fell in the very low range. These deficits, I thought, did not bode well for vocational success. Not wanting to raise hopes only to disappoint Jimmy and his mother, I thought it best that he continue to gain skills before he came to the program.

"However, because of Connie Cronin's conviction that Jimmy's Type A personality would help him succeed, Jimmy entered my program, the North River Collaborative's Educational Work Experience Program (EWEP), and he became my greatest teacher. Jimmy showed me that a keen, unwavering memory, a wonderful sense of humor and sheer determination were qualities to also consider for vocational success. These traits and Jimmy's near immediate successes led me to reevaluate the standards I had previously set and helped me expand my own horizons to work more effectively with other students who were more cognitively impaired.

"Jimmy needed clear, defined steps; ones that were modeled, monitored and honed. With that, his talents sparkle. It was through consistent, year-long job coaching and eliciting the help from fellow employees on site that led to his employment as a custodian in a family-run warehouse for office supplies called Nelson Copy. Jimmy became one of their most beloved workers."

A Sigh of Relief for Me, Maturation for Jimmy

Starting out in his new program, his new teacher, Anne, told me that given the fact that we had only five years instead of the normal six to prepare him, the days of academic programming would take a second seat to vocational work. And work, it turns out, is what Jimmy loves and where he excels. I remember the program emphasizing the word "thorough" with him. To this day when *I* say it, he might bristle, but he gets it! Jimmy is happiest when he can see accomplishment: emptying the dishwasher, stacking wood, raking leaves, weeding, cleaning out the garage, to name a few. Jimmy has his father's stamina and his drive. Later, that was to draw the two of them together.

Jimmy showed a unique and mature work ethic in these later adolescent years, but I was curious to know his overall maturation level. How did I find this out? I asked him if he had a girlfriend. For a while he said, "No." However, when it came time for the spring prom at a nearby hotel, Jimmy was excited to go. He liked imitating his brothers getting all dressed up; in particular, he liked new shoes. He soon had quite a crush on a classmate, Jennifer, and she had a little crush on him. Jimmy enjoyed the role of the boyfriend; somehow, he knew just what to do. He liked to sit on the couch with his arm around her and give her little kisses. He also loved slow dancing! When other people would dance with Jennifer, he didn't seem to mind. For unknown reasons, that romance ended and yet Jimmy and she are still friendly when they see each other.

Then came Nadine. She, too, had Down syndrome. Her brother, Mitchell also with Down syndrome, was dating my friend's daughter with special needs. My friend thought that Jimmy should consider taking out Nadine, making it a foursome. Nadine was a few years older, but she was part of a group familiar to Jimmy. For their first date, we took the four of them to the 99 Restaurant and Pub for dinner; they were in one booth, we in another. Preparing to leave after a nice dinner, Jimmy helped Nadine on with her coat, opened the door for her, and took her by the elbow to walk her to the car. Nadine, in her theatrical, dead-pan style, said, "Oh my, I have landed a gentleman this time." A few minutes later from the back seat, I heard her say, "Mmmm...Nadine Cronin...I like the sound of that. What would you think of me as your daughter-in-law, Mrs. Cronin?" "I would be very proud to have you as a daughter-in-law, Nadine." Jimmy just laughed. They would sit in the back seat and, every once in a while, he would pull her over for a kiss. When we arrived at Nadine's house, Jimmy walked her to the door. In the future, if he was going to pick her up to take her somewhere, or even bring her back over to our house to go swimming, he would say, "Can I stop and get her flowers?" He had manners that he must have seen on television. The Nadine and Jim duo went on for some time.

Though he had come miles and was now successfully employed three days a week at Nelson Copy, Jimmy showed great trepidation anticipating his graduation from high school. He was nervous about not having a place to go every day. He loved school; he loved his peers, he loved his teachers, and he loved striving for "Worker of the Month." Overall, he loved the challenges and the successes, all of which rebuilt his self-esteem. Life in school was familiar after five years, and he knew what was expected of him. He did not want to let go of that safety net. His brothers had graduated and moved on and everyone was telling him that this is part of life – but Jimmy was grieving, his tears on graduation day were real. It was not the friendships he would miss; he does not seem to have or want friendships with other kids with special needs. Instead, he was sad to lose the experience of being part of a group where he knew he belonged.

The day of his graduation, I basked in the light, knowing just how far Jimmy had come. I was so proud of him. He had proved that he could shine in school, at a workplace, with girls and certainly at home with his two brothers. The following is his brother Kevin's college essay, written in 1998, which says it all.

Reflections: My Brother
By Kevin Cronin

"My oldest brother, Jimmy, is 23 years old and was born with Down syndrome. When Jimmy was born he had a lot of health problems. Since doctors didn't know much about kids with Down syndrome then they all said he was most likely going to die and, if he did live, he would never be able to walk or be independent. Even priests who talked to my mother told her to let him die, but my parents refused.

"Growing up was very difficult for Jimmy. Simple things that people take for granted were tough for him – tying his shoes, zipping a jacket or writing his name. Jim's speech was also poor and many people had trouble understanding what he said. I first started noticing that Jimmy was different from other kids when I was very young. An easy task such as hanging up a shirt would only take me five seconds, but it would take Jimmy a minute or two. Then there were the neighborhood whiffle ball games; Jimmy was never able to hit, or the football games where he could never catch a pass, but he never gave up or lost confidence. My neighbors respected him for that and treated him like he was one of the guys.

"With all the odds stacked against him, Jimmy went through every day with a positive attitude and a strong determination to complete the tasks that were set in front of him. Jimmy never used his disabilities as an excuse to get out of work. Being born with poor motor skills, he was physically unable to grip a pencil the correct way and write legibly. Jimmy spent many hours at night, however, practicing his typing skills. Typing did not come easy for Jimmy either. Because of his poor coordination, he would often press keys that he never meant to but with practice and his strong will to succeed, Jimmy mastered this skill and used it often in place of writing.

"Jimmy is now 23 and holds a job nearby that he walks to every day. He cleans two floors of a major business office and six bathrooms. Then he comes home and vacuums our house to help out my mother. Jimmy has influenced my life so much. He has taught me patience and has made me an all-around better person. When things get tough for me whether it is on the sports field, in the classroom or in the gym, I just think of my brother and how much he's overcome and how much easier I have it than he does. That's all the motivation I need.

81

"I think, in a world where it's so easy to give up and make excuses, Jimmy is a great inspiration for us all."

New Fun Times

Jimmy did settle into a new routine. He had work during the day, a bowling league he played on once a week, and sports to watch on TV, which he adores. He is such a fan of all sports and is fanatical about keeping up with all of them. One night I happened on a show that got *me* all pumped up. It featured a baseball team for special needs kids called the Challengers. Hmmmmm, I thought, since Jim coaches our other two boys in baseball and coaches All-Star teams for the town, why not ask him to help start a Challenger team for Jimmy. I proposed it, but he flat-out refused to even consider it. For one thing, he did not see any merit in *anyone* playing baseball who could not perform at the All-Star level, so for him to think of Jimmy playing baseball at all was, in his mind, preposterous. I wanted this so much for Jimmy I could taste it, so I pressed Jim. "The town's youth association will help; we can do this!" Trying to abruptly stop this conversation, he said, "You are not doing this, and I am not doing this. I am not comfortable with this population." I was taken aback. "This *is* your population; how can you say that?" "I don't *like* this population; I won't do it." That was that; the truth had finally been spoken.

However, things have a funny way of working out. One of Jim's best friends, Gerry, was an All-Star coach for Jim's rival team in town. The two of them would fight and squabble to no end over All-Star issues as if they were coaching major leagues.

Gerry happened to become the commissioner of the town's youth athletic association and came to me out of the blue asking if I would like to get a team together for Jimmy. "I sure would," I said and told him what I knew about the Challengers. By this time, I had learned that the Challengers is actually an official but separate division under Little League (developed in 1989). "Well," he said, "talk to my wife Patty and we'll help you get it going." Patty, a wonderful person and the force behind the force, was on board immediately. We first needed to field two teams, since there were no other Challengers in the area to play against. We contacted at least ten special education directors from every school in a 20 miles radius and got an overwhelmingly positive response. As things moved along, Gerry one day approached my husband and said, excitedly, "We're going to do this Challenger thing; it will be awesome. Connie put the paperwork in, got two teams lined up, petitioned the youth association for uniforms and it's now official – we're Little League Challengers. We even lucked out getting the fields we wanted." Peer pressure worked. Jim was in.

Thanks to Gerry, I was appointed the Commissioner of the Challenger Division. Now, all we needed was a pitcher and a catcher. The answer couldn't be clearer; Jim was an excellent pitcher, he couldn't refuse. Gerry became the catcher. Patty coached one team and I coached the other. Now mind you, neither Patty nor I knew anything about baseball. I might add that we were about as athletic as a house plant. Consequently, we were hit by foul balls constantly and for years walked around with painful bruises because we were not agile enough to get out of the way. But we learned.

Our two teams represented the spectrum of disabilities: mentally retarded, blind, cerebral palsy and other physical issues, as well as emotional and behavioral problems. It was actually frightening to think of giving some of these kids a bat. Looking carefully at the ramifications of each disability, we had to devise ways to get certain people around the bases. The answer? Every special athlete, we decided, had to have a buddy, an athlete from an active sports team in town. Both Gerry and Jim "persuaded" their All-Star players to assist us by telling them that they would sit on the bench unless they showed up every Sunday night. So, now we had these top athletes committed to help, but I still needed as many buddies as I could find for people like Karen, who is blind and needed two people to walk her from base to base. In the end, we solicited all of Gerry's family, all my family, and all the kids in our neighborhood. We needed buddies for our emotionally troubled athletes, so I went to the police station and asked for kids who needed community service hours. Some tough cookies showed up, but they were perfect. If an athlete kicked sand at someone, that community service kid kicked it right back. It all worked.

According to Little League by-laws, the Challenger Division starts at age seven or eight and goes to age 22. However, because it took so much time to get this off the ground, most of the kids were close to 20, so we loosened the rules and simply extended the "retirement" age. On other things, however, I was very strict. Parents were not allowed on the field unless they were substitutes for someone who didn't show up, or we needed an able body to catch balls that were headed towards an athlete's head. No parent was allowed to speak to their son or daughter while we played, and they certainly weren't allowed to coach. Athletes were to listen to Coach Connie or Coach Patty only.

Everything had to be very well thought out. We would go through the lineup at each inning and reverse it the following inning to eliminate too much bench sitting. Two rules were: no outs and no strikes. Any athlete could have 300 swings at a ball if they needed it. If a batter became discouraged, he or she would get some help using either hand-over-hand or the T-stand we would bring.

I was eager to watch my husband in his new role as pitcher, as he was a very demanding and emotional coach with his All-Star teams. I got the surprise of a lifetime.

I mean this from the bottom of my heart when I say that Jim's calling in life was to pitch to these kids. Watching him interact with Gerry on the field brought some heartwarming moments. The two of them, usually so competitive and so accustomed to cut-throat baseball, were incredulous watching these athletes play ball. Neither Jim nor Gerry could fathom why members of the team in the field would be rooting for the person at bat. "C'mon," hit it over my head, right over here," a fielder would say. This of course, lightened everyone's mood and it turned Jim's and Gerry's heads around.

I was also consoled seeing Jim start to connect with a few special needs athletes. Jim learned which ones he could joke around with, usually the kids who were too big for their britches. One of the sassier athletes would get up to bat saying, "Hey, Fatty doesn't know how to pitch," and Jim would have a good time throwing him ball after ball. When the game was over, I would remind Jim of the fun. I would encourage him and emphasize, "These *are* your people, they adore you." He might say, "Did you see so and so hit?" I would answer, "Did you see Jimmy throw?"

Jimmy played short stop quite a bit; he was good, really good. He would charge the ball and make the play. Of course, the other kids didn't usually catch it, but Jimmy always knew where the play was. He was also a power hitter, often parlaying his hit into a home run with creative base running; he knew the real rules of baseball.

I would often put Jimmy out into center field. He would get the ball and with such a strong arm could throw it right into the catcher's glove. However, since the rule for the Challengers is "No Outs," the catcher was instructed to drop the ball. Good naturedly, Jimmy would shout out, "Time for a new catcher!" Fans and parents spoke of how well Jimmy played, which, of course, delighted me.

Sports are Jimmy's passion, but he also enjoys social events, especially parties. For a while now, he has been part of a social club in Norwell. Each October, they have a Halloween party; costumes have always been optional. Only once, when I worked for a hospital, did Jimmy dress up. He went as a doctor – in scrubs, with a mask and, of course, rubber gloves. Other years he has not wanted to wear anything but his football jerseys. But last year, he declared that he wanted to be a girl. His brothers said, "That's crazy, just be a football player." Nope, he was going to be a girl. I had more fun picking that outfit out at the discount store, Building 19. It was all very fashionable with a size 2X skirt, a big, curly blond wig, a gargantuan string of pearls, and a huge, hideous purse. To top it off, Jimmy wore his black high-top sneakers. The house was brought down when he arrived in my mother's full length, mink coat. Staff were flabbergasted. "What are you doing letting him wear your mink coat?" "I don't wear it. He can wear it every day if he wants to."

On our way to the party in my bright, red Cadillac we got caught in a construction site. Construction workers, I noticed, always seemed to look closely at a red Cadillac. From a distance, they spotted this floozy looking, boofed-up blond in the passenger seat with her window wide open. With great hopes and bulging eyeballs, they leaned on their shovels eagerly waiting until we came along. Naturally, I had to slow down to get through the actual construction and we watched as their rascally excited faces morphed into unconcealed horror. Kidding Jimmy, I said, "They're making eyes at you. They're going to want your phone number." He dissolved into laughter. He always appreciates a good joke, especially if he is a participant.

A Miracle in Our Lives

Humor is really the elixir in life, and in Jimmy's case it was the ingredient that built bridges and salved all wounds.

Seismic shifts began to occur in our house when Jimmy was out of school for three years. He was now 25 years old and still working at Nelson Copy. For one, our household shrank as Brendan and Kevin both went off to college. My husband's favorite phrase was, "It's just the three of us. That's how we like it, Jimmy, just the three of us." But you could see the pained look of loneliness on Jimmy's face every time it was said; his best buddies were gone – he was bereft.

Things had changed for Jim and me as well. I was extremely busy working two jobs. Jim traveled a lot less, so he was home more and continued to be involved in multiple projects around the house. Jimmy's work days ended at 2 or 3 pm, so when the two were home together, Jimmy simply followed his father around looking for ways to be useful. He would always start by getting Jim a beer, even without being asked. Then he would be summoned to stand nearby and hold his hand out, full of whatever it was his father needed: nails to fix a fence, a paint can, a shovel he would use eventually. Jimmy would do anything just to be with him; always silent, always attentive.

Jimmy's steady presence continued quietly for many months. In time, they began this foolish bantering. "You're crazy," one would say. The other would answer, "No, you're crazy." Back and forth it would go for hours, accompanied by heaps of giggles on Jimmy's part. Their repartee grew to include: "You don't know." "I don't know what?" "You don't know Jack." "I know Jack, he lives next door." Slowly, and invisibly, this routine began to stitch them together.

When Jim would go off to Home Depot, Jimmy would simply slip into the car's passenger seat to go with him. I, of course, was nervous thinking Jim would be oblivious to Jimmy's needs. I would shout from the doorway, "Watch him in the parking lot. He doesn't know safety around cars." Recollecting our own so-called "family outings," I had visions of Jim losing Jimmy. Whenever we all went anywhere, Jim would be 50 steps ahead of us.

As the months went on, Jimmy began to do whatever he could to be with his father. He never had an agenda of his own, he just wanted to share time and space with his dad. Soon they started going on errands to places like Lowe's and Ocean State Job Lot. Each time they made it home safely with no missing child reports.

For 20 years in our house, Jim had insisted on bringing home Chinese food on Friday nights. I finally made it known that I did not like Chinese food and did not want to eat it anymore. Jim announced then that *he* would go to the China Plaza and eat there. Jimmy piped up, "Can I go?" Jim would order a beer at the bar; Jimmy a Diet Coke. In no time, they would find a beer waiting on the bar for Jim when they walked in and a Diet Coke for Jimmy. I went with them one night and when we walked in the door the staff blurted out, "Jimmy's here!"

They became a kind of twosome, broadening out to local places like CVS where another of their routines began. Jim would walk straight to the blood pressure machine, stick his arm in and, after it was read, he would go off to get his prescriptions or whatever else he was in there for. Then Jimmy would march over and put his arm in to take his own blood pressure. No words had to be exchanged. Jimmy just watched and did what Jim did.

A relationship was finally forming between them. I always knew that Jim loved Jimmy; in fact, he loved all his children. But there was a lot of performance involved for any of us to be loved by Jim, and Jimmy was always willing to do whatever it took. He would get Jim another beer, he would hold the hammer, he would move yards and yards of dirt; he would stand for hours doing anything, unlike Jim's other sons who would complain or ask a hundred times when this would be over. Not Jimmy.

Since Jim was home more during the week, he decided to take over the grocery shopping and would take Jimmy with him whenever he was home. This was helpful for me with my new workload. Every once in a while, I would ask Jim to drive Jimmy somewhere – Monday night bowling, for example. Jim did not like to do this, but he did it periodically if I had to work.

If Jimmy came down with a bad cold or had an ear infection when I was working, I would tell Jim that I could leave work, but I would not get paid. Taking Jimmy to a doctor was clearly out of Jim's comfort zone, but when he finally had to take him he asked me, "Where do I go, who do I talk to, what do I say? I don't know what to do." After managing the first time, the doctor's office began seeing more of Jim than me.

Having assistance gave me a bit of wiggle room; it meant I did not have to be in ten places at once. Keep in mind that Jim did not do the heavy lifting, like cleaning up after Jimmy threw up all over the floor. Instead, he would call me at work and say, "Clean up on aisle four." I never minded, I would just answer, "Put paper towels over it, I will do it when I get home." I was grateful for the help.

Brendan walked into the house once when Jimmy was home sick and heard Jim yelling at Jimmy for having diarrhea. "Are you going to do this all day long? Can't you stop it, this house smells like crap. Your mother is going to come home to this disgusting smell." Jimmy just laughed, but Brendan was horrified and spoke up, telling his father not to talk to Jimmy that way. To this day, Jimmy will imitate his father, "I don't want my house smelling like crap," and he giggles the way only Jimmy can. Jimmy could turn these horrors, these "Jim eruptions" around, always with laugher.

Another time, Jim was outside barking orders at Jimmy. Jim was not explicit enough in his requests. This time he told Jimmy to "get the hose." Well, Jimmy went and got a hose, but what he picked up was the soaker hose that Jim had just spent hours meticulously placing all around my garden. Jimmy simply pulled it all up and lugged it over. Jim, purple with fury, yelled, "Not thaaat one!" Brendan stepped up again, telling Jim not to yell at Jimmy. Jimmy, however, responded to his father's reaction with gales of laughter while repeating, "Not thaaat one, the OTHER one." All Jim could do was say, "Look at this, now I have to go and do this all over again." At that point, Jimmy would be bent over laughing while trying to help Jim bring the soaker hose back to the garden. Laughter is contagious and, in this case, it curtailed my husband's anger. There were times when Jim could walk in and announce lightheartedly, "You'll never guess what *your* son did." Even today, if I ask Jimmy for a spoon and he brings the wrong size, I will correct him and he will say back to me, with his father's intonations, "NOT thaaat one," laughing his way back to the drawer to get the right one.

Jimmy's chortle just diffuses the bombs; confrontations are simply eliminated. One day, in an effort to be helpful and to keep busy, Jimmy decided to vacuum the family room floor. I had just sat down on the couch with a magazine and warned him to be careful of the vacuum around the coffee table. "Don't knock the statues over." He went along in his merry way and, sure enough, bumped the table beheading a statue or two. I was angry, especially after having had this discussion with him on more than this occasion. The vacuum was still running so, to get his attention, I slapped him on the shoulder. "Didn't I just tell you?" He looked at me without emotion, finished vacuuming and then sat down on the couch, quiet for a good long time. Then he turned to me. "How's your hand?" he asked stone-faced. "Fine, thank you very much," I retorted. "How's your shoulder?" By now, he was beside himself with laughter; I lost the discipline of the moment. How can you continue to be angry at someone who is laughing or mimicking you in a respectful way?

If there is ever tension or even competition, Jimmy has a way to diffuse it. Once the neighborhood kids were playing a game and an argument ensued about what constituted a point in this competition. It got a bit heated until Jimmy went up to one of them and said, "Don't worry about it, he throws like a girl." The whole group of players just burst out laughing. The dispute was over.

Time and time again I saw how Jimmy worked magic, especially with Jim. It is Jimmy's way and it is Jimmy's gift. He's always had a sense of humor; he was silly and goofy as a youngster, which made it hard to discipline at times. People now perceive him as being fairly serious, but he was always a really happy kid. He did get more solemn when he got into Ernie's room, but that's because he was dormant in there; he just lost his spark. I saw him blossom again in his high school classroom and then again in these few years with his father. Their silly skits and time together sustained them, and with that came the brightening of Jimmy's soul. They soon became inseparable. Wherever you saw Jim – the front yard, back yard, side yard – you saw Jimmy.

After all these years, my husband was finally able to see through Down syndrome to appreciate Jimmy's incredible assets; physical strength for one. One joint project was redoing one of the bathrooms, and Jim watched as Jimmy picked up and carried the toilet out from the basement on his own. He is as strong as a bull and his father liked that.

Another time, Jimmy, without flinching, picked up our dryer and held it while Jim laid a new floor underneath. I pleaded but he would not put that dryer down. Jim valued that. He began to see Jimmy's determination and his stick-to-itiveness. He also loved the fact that Jimmy never left his side. My husband had found a cooperative chum who gave him what he wanted. His other boys were always rushing to get through and telling him all the things they had to do. Jimmy was never too busy.

Little by little, Jimmy was measuring up to Jim's standards. A few years into this new relationship, my husband decided to expand our deck and I saw Jim, for the very first time, instruct *and* help Jimmy. Using hand over hand, Jimmy and he drilled many of the pieces together. After endless weeks of hard work, Jimmy turned to his father and proudly, but a bit unsure, said, "I built that deck." Jim responded, "Yes, you did. *You* built that deck." The tides had finally turned.

June 8th

Jimmy's work at Nelson Copy came to an end when they closed the doors on Friday, June 6, 2008. The next Monday he was to start full time at a new adult day program in an adjoining town. This was another transition for Jimmy and it felt to him like leaving school – a big loss. He had grown comfortable at Nelson; he knew the routine, he felt important and the employees loved him. I decided to ease his distress with a party – a retirement party, I called it – and scheduled it for that Sunday, June 8.

Despite the torturous heat and humidity, I did this celebration up big, inviting all the family and, of course, Jimmy's girlfriend, Nadine. I got the food for a grand cookout, ordered a special cake, and hung lots of balloons. After hours in the pool just trying to stay cool, we retreated to the shade on the deck. Jimmy, Nadine and Jim went inside, but soon Jimmy joined us back on the deck looking a bit glum. Nadine apparently had switched the channel from Jim and Jimmy's beloved Red Sox game to gospel singers. Jimmy just muttered under his breath and left the room while Jim hollered to have her turn the TV back, but she was not shaken and stayed her course, insisting she was "the guest." Jim then screamed at me to get the clicker from her, but I reinforced Nadine's truth – she *was* the guest. Nadine was a force to be reckoned with and she usually got her way. She was never rude, but very strong willed; in fact, she ran our household.

Nadine and my husband finally came outside and we all sat having our cake and ice cream, but there wasn't a word coming from Jimmy. I finally turned to him and said, "You're awfully quiet. Are you feeling okay?" "I have a girl ache," he replied. "Whaaaat?" I asked. "I have a girl ache!" "What's a girl ache?" "It's like a headache from a girl." "Well, do I give you a girl ache?" "No." My daughter-in-law, Kerry, asked, "Do I give you a girl ache?" "No." Nadine then piped up, saying, "I guess that leaves me!" "Yes," Jimmy said, "you give me a girl ache." That was that. For whatever reason, he had been pushed over the edge; he was done with Nadine. No confrontation, no argument; it was just over. "Well, don't worry about it, Nadine," I said. "He's probably tired or nervous about his new job." I ended the party saying, "Jimmy, let's take Nadine home." "I am not going," he replied. Then he walked over to her and said "Goodbye." No kiss, just goodbye. He then turned around and proceeded upstairs. On the way home, Nadine spoke up.

"Guess it's sayonara for me!" They still see each other at various events and, happily, there is no friction between them.

I returned from dropping Nadine off and came back to find Jim and Jimmy standing on the deck trying to find a cool breeze. It was still so sultry. I suggested we go up to the bedroom, put on the only air conditioner and watch the Celtics playoff game together. "No, we are going to watch it in our 'lucky' seats," Jim said, as they headed to their recliners in the living room. This had become a familiar sight, a sight etched in my mind's eye forever. Between the debilitating heat and waiting on everyone at Jimmy's party, I was so exhausted I climbed the stairs and fell into bed. The one regret I have from that day is that I didn't kiss my husband goodnight. He was to die within hours.

I woke at 2:30 in the morning and tried to feel for Jim next to me, but he was not there. He often fell asleep in his recliner. My role was to go downstairs and pull him up saying, "C'mon, come to bed." He would answer, "Don't wake me, I'm *in* bed." He had a CPAP machine and I worried when he did not use it. But 2:30 in the morning was much later than usual. I had a funny feeling. I headed down and opened the door at the bottom of the stairs to a full view of Jim's chair. I stopped in mid-step at the sight of him, paler than I had ever seen anyone. I then raced to him. He was ice cold despite the humid 90-degree temperature. I tried to wake him; he was not asleep. I then attempted CPR, but, when I couldn't budge him, I called 911. It felt like I waited forever, but more than likely they arrived in minutes. Our two Golden Retrievers *always* slept upstairs with Jimmy, never downstairs, but now they surrounded Jim's chair and would not move.

When the paramedics came I literally had to pull the dogs away. Things seemed to move in slow motion. While they took the screen door off its hinges to get the gurney out, I called Brendan, only to get his wife, Kerry. "Get Brendan over here, now!" I said. I did not say what was wrong. Poor Brendan panicked, thinking there was a problem with Jimmy and came onto our street on one wheel. By then the paramedics were trying to resuscitate Jim in the ambulance parked in our driveway. Brendan began fighting to get in the ambulance. His voice high pitched, he said, "I live here, is that my brother?" No answer came. "IS THAT MY BROTHER?" Brendan's voice crescendoed. Still nothing. "IS SOMETHING WRONG WITH MY BROTHER?" he screamed; he was beside himself. One of the paramedics opened the door and said, "I think it's your Dad, we need to work on him. Go to your mother. She's in the house." Brendan and Kerry came in. By then I had called my girlfriend, Kathy, who was on her way over with her husband. Kerry pushed me upstairs knowing I had to get dressed. We then heard the paramedic tell Brendan that his father was going to the hospital and we were to follow. "What about Jimmy?" was all I thought to ask. Kathy's husband said he would stay until Jimmy woke up.

I decided not to call Kevin in the middle of the night and wait instead until 6 or 6:30 am; after all, he lived in South Boston and I wanted to spare him the drive down and let him sleep in case Jim was alive. Reality, however, became a bit blurry and surreal; I actually started to think that Jim had had a heart attack and would end up recovering in the hospital. Brendan called his brother anyway only to hear Kevin say, "I don't know how many times I expected this phone call."

Once in the hospital, we were ushered into a separate, small, dingy room away from the regular waiting room. It had no windows, the paint was drab, and it held only a few straight-backed chairs. A minister came to see us. I remember talking to him about *his* ministry and encouraging him in *his* work, clearly not processing what had just happened, convinced that Jim was going to be okay. I must have known the truth deep down, but when the door opened and I heard the words, "Your husband passed away," I went into shock. The doctor asked if we wanted to go in to see him, and the four of us went in together. My sons were uncomfortable, but I reached out to Jim and touched him one last time.

By the time we got home it was early morning, and we sat watching the sun come up, drinking coffee on our deck and waiting to hear Jimmy stir. The thought of telling Jimmy this news made me physically sick; I was never more nervous in my life. Brendan and Kevin would not let me go upstairs to hold him; they waited until they heard Jimmy thud down the stairs and then went to him, leaving me in the living room. I cannot say I fought to go.

They all met on the stairs, those same stairs they had grown up on; the stairs they pushed each other down in boxes, the stairs on which their little feet pitter-pattered up and down, all day long. I do not know what his brothers said, but I heard a long, shrill sound and then a loud shriek. I was frozen until I heard another drawn out wail and a louder cry, and then Jimmy's torturous sobs. I ran to him.

How do you get death through your head when you have just watched the Celtics game together the night before? How do you understand finality when you still see the glass of water you left next to your father's chair – the glass you *always* left for him before you went to bed at night? Typically, Jimmy would take the wine glass out of Jim's hands if he was asleep and put it next to the sink, then fill a glass of water for Jim to take up with him. But there the glass remained, the water untouched. Jimmy's heart was shocked, and it was broken.

Somehow, the world went on that morning and the van for Jimmy's new program pulled up to get him. Brendan went out to talk to the driver, telling him that Jimmy would not be starting for a week. At this point, I was on automatic. My minister came, I remember, and two friends appeared. Those two women sat on the deck the entire, sweltering day. Like sitting Shiva, they were there for me. I do not remember feeding them or even offering them anything to drink, they just sat. One of the women, who had lost her husband the year before, told Kevin that she would call the funeral parlor and have the director come to the house to plan the service. I sat in a stupor but functioned when needed; Jimmy was in and out of the house. I found myself afraid of saying anything in front of him; I wanted to sidestep this process. All I wanted was to take his pain away.

One detail I recall was ordering a limousine for six people. The funeral director kept saying five. I insisted it was six, thinking he might be excluding my daughter-in-law. I spoke up, saying, "She's my daughter-in-law; she's part of my family and she's going with us." Turns out they *were* counting correctly; I was including Jim. After counting family members three or four times, I finally got it. The reality took my breath away; Jim was really gone.

The night of the wake, Jimmy decided he did not want to see his father in a box, so a close friend took him to her house where they cooked out and rented movies. He did, however, go to the funeral.

My pastor, unaccustomed to having funeral services in our church, bolstered me, saying we will create one and he did – it was perfect. So many people came. Jimmy, Kevin, Brendan and Kerry sat with me in the front row. We remained stoic until a young girl in our congregation stood to sing a beautiful song, made more beautiful by her a cappella voice. Jimmy's flood gates burst; he came apart. All 200 attendees wept, heartbroken for Jimmy. My two other boys were pall bearers, but I wanted Jimmy to stay and help me out of the church. However, at the end of the service, without any nudging or instruction, Jimmy stood right up, went to an open spot next to the casket and, as though it had been planned, stoically escorted his father out of the church with his brothers. There were no words at the cemetery for either Jimmy or me, just tears.

That night, Jimmy announced that he was going to sleep with me. I assumed he did not want to be alone, so I agreed. For three nights Jimmy stayed with me and then, finally, he said, "Can I go back to my own bed? Will you be okay?" Only then did I realize he was doing this for me.

This, then, began the journey of healing.

Our New Life

Things were foggy for a long time. I remember knowing where Jimmy was, but I did not know what he was doing. He began his new day program. Talk about courage. I could not have done that; I could not go back to work for weeks. I do not know how I expected him to function, but the people at his day program embraced him. They told him they knew what had happened and said he could come to anyone of them if he needed to. He spent a lot of time crying. I think we both went in and out of shock, but I would be surprised if anyone in the family has a clear recollection of those weeks.

As we tried to carry on with everyday life and put time behind us, so many things in our house started to go wrong. Within two weeks after Jim's death, the pump for the pool just blew, flooding everywhere; mice were even pouring out of the tool shed; it was a nightmare. Little things happened, too, that led to bigger problems. I tried to chlorinate the pool and could not get the top off, so I could not clean the pool. I called our pool company contact, who said, "I have been trying to talk Jim into buying a new pump for years." "Go ahead," I said, "Put it in." I just wanted it all taken care of.

Jimmy also remembers the time shortly after that when it *rained* in the dining room. I never knew that gutters had to be cleaned out; that was not in *my* manual. Turns out they were badly clogged and when a rainstorm hit, water poured into the dining room all over my hardwood floors, my beautiful antique curtains and Jim's teakwood desk, with all his papers still sitting there from months ago. Despite hollering for Jimmy to get me beach towels, sheets, tablecloths, etc., the water got deeper by the minute. I was not making any headway, and finally sat down in the middle of the soaked floor and just cried. Jimmy came and simply stood by my side, patting my shoulder. To this day he asks, "Do you remember when it rained in the dining room?" "Oh yes, I do," I answer.

I also had to have the whole septic replaced a few months later. That was a big enough job, made bigger when the workers forgot to hook the system back up to my bathroom. After four or five days of flushing, the pipes ruptured and a 10- to 15-foot geyser sprung up in the backyard. Not only did it erupt outside, but a huge backlog of waste burst through the bathroom floor and flooded the bathroom and my bedroom.

I felt bombarded. I did not know how to fix anything. I was beginning to wonder what all this pandemonium was telling me.

When winter came around, heating propane was delivered. The driver said, "What happened here? I have always had a path cleared for me right to the backyard." Furious and insulted, I fired back. "Pardon me, my snow shoveler has just died." He then said, "Well, I'll do it." But, in the end, he could not find the tank buried in the ten feet of snow, so he threw the shovel in the yard and left. My empty tank remained empty despite the frigid temperatures. It was those kinds of things that made me feel so stupid. I did not know any of the house particulars – Jim did. I would stand in the bay window in tears.

Sitting on our deck one day, I mentioned to Jimmy that I was thinking of selling the house. He quickly said, "I will fight you." Jimmy's tone was adamant. I told him that we would absolutely not move unless *he* wanted to. "So, don't be afraid that I am going to do something you don't want, but how would it be if we went together to look?" With each house we entered, I put the focus on him and he began to get excited by the prospect of a new bedroom set. Without a definite place in mind, we began accumulating things for his new room; he could pick out anything he wanted. The house I fell in love with had a long and open staircase. I was afraid Jimmy would not be able to manage it, but Brendan brought him to the model home and practiced going up and down the stairs a few times. He came back to me saying, "He's fine!"

We had an errand to do at CVS that day and I watched as Jimmy headed straight for the blood pressure machine, stuck his arm in and waited for the readout. It seemed a bit humorous to me until I looked over at the pharmacist who, with tears in his eyes, told me of the memorable routine he had observed each time my husband came in with Jimmy. I said nothing to Jimmy other than to ask how his blood pressure was, to which he responded, "Fine." I am quite sure he never learned to read it. Jimmy and I had one last chat about whether to move in the parking lot of CVS. "We don't have to do this." I began. "We don't have to move. We don't have to do anything. If you don't want to do this, you tell me now and I will not sell the house." He said, "I think you should sell the house." "Why?" "So that we don't have to be sad all the time. I don't want to be here anymore." I put the house on the market in June 2009. It sold in 2010, almost two years to the day after Jim died.

Jimmy said a lot of goodbyes to things at our family home: the fence he helped mend, the deck *he* built, the yard he raked faithfully, and the pool he vacuumed and cleaned – all things he did with his father. Every time I turned around in that house for the two years after Jim died, I would see my husband walk up from behind the big, old oak tree or the blue spruce. I am sure Jimmy saw him too; Jim's presence was palpable.

Finally, in July, we moved into our new home and, together, took a deep breath. It feels like home. The neighbors have reached out and Jimmy has already met a new male mentor and friend. I knew things were going to be okay when Jimmy turned to me one day and said, "It's just the two of us now. That's how I like it, Mom, just the two of us."

Reflections: Post Script

After Jim died I sought counseling to deal with the whirlwind of conflicting emotions and the years of having to battle for the life I wanted for my family. I also wanted my boys to see the strong person who emerged. I see them quite a bit now and when they do come, they are here to visit and share their lives. I feel the lightness. They do not have to make me feel okay and I do not need their pity or protection anymore. Happily, the anger they grew up with has not been carried over into their adulthood. In fact, both boys approach their role as husband and father with a gentle kindness that exudes love. I am so grateful.

I still feel enormously blessed by Jimmy, though I cannot say that "I'm out of the woods." Even though he is nearly 42 years old, worry is still a constant. Being Jim's mom means getting up every morning to try and make sense out of the pieces of a jigsaw puzzle. You think they fit together, but the next day you have ten more pieces and a very different picture. I try daily to grasp the real picture of what is going on with him, mostly because Jimmy does not communicate well. For example, he will say on a Sunday, "My throat hurts." "Oh really, when did it start to hurt?" "Friday." "Friday? And you didn't tell me?" "I didn't want to worry you" or "I wanted to go to (such and such event)." Once, he went to camp with a double ear infection. He was so sick but didn't want to miss out, so did not tell me.

For so long, I was in such fear that Jimmy was going to die that I could not ignore anything. With other kids you can often ignore a bellyache, but with Jimmy a bellyache could easily turn into a life-threatening situation. An ear infection for a typical kid is just that, but as soon as I see Jimmy scratching his ear, or when his ear turns a little red, I am at the doctors. Once, when he was young, I watched one of his ears change from pink to beet red over the course of a day. This infection had been treated for a week, but when I called the office to describe the worsening situation, they sloughed it off, saying, "Well, he still has medication left. Keep up with that and let it run its course." By 5 pm, it was clear that he could not go through the night, so I drove to the ENT's office. I knew staff was still there, despite it being after hours; I also knew there was only one way out of the office. Jimmy's ear stood straight out at a 90-degree angle, and, by now, it was firetruck red. I stood in the hallway, banging on the door and yelling, "I know you people are in there and I know you have families, but you are not getting out unless you climb out a window. Somebody has to see my son."

I pounded for a long time and when the door finally opened, I said I wanted to see Dr. Hyde. I was told he had finished office hours. "He will not be leaving 'til he sees this ear," I said, trying to remain calm. "Just take him to the emergency room," they insisted. "No, he is treated here; I am here, and the doctor's here. He's going to see him." I will never forget Dr. Hyde's face when he finally came out and took one look at Jimmy. "Oh, my God," he shrieked, "bring him in my office." He jabbed a wick in this very infected ear and drained it while Jimmy screamed in pain.

Overall, Jimmy has never enjoyed good health and gets sick well over six times a year. His illnesses last for weeks and affect his mood and his ability to participate in his program, work and recreational activities. I do not know how well he hears either; reports indicate he has "moderate" hearing loss.

As a baby, Jimmy did not cry much. Even when he got hurt from falling he did not cry; he would just stand or sit there looking bewildered and stunned. And today, we could be sitting at a table with a group and I will hear a slight grunt from Jimmy. I know this means he has to go to the bathroom. I will say, "You have to learn to excuse yourself or come over and tap me on the shoulder rather than sit there and be uncomfortable." He is still not good at expressing what he needs.

If I am crying, he will comfort me. He will pat my back or give me hugs. If he fears he has made me mad or done something wrong, his voice will start to shake and he will look like he is going to cry. I will say, "You look like you're going to cry," and sometimes he does.

Jimmy is extremely sensitive to death. He cried when his dog Max died and when his uncle Arthur died, and he was overcome with tears at his Nana's funeral. Music in a church now will sometimes resonate and provoke tears. He keeps himself so stoic so much of the time that when he lets down it is almost a surprise to him.

Jimmy can sometimes gush with tears. It can seem as though they are not going to stop and other people, including his brothers, are frightened by this intense display of emotion, fearing they won't know what to do. After his father died, Jimmy burst several times a day, but he was able to regain composure after each intense session. His crying usually made me cry. Afterwards, we would both feel better.

Looking back, I really do understand how some people cannot keep up the hyper-vigilance I needed for Jimmy. There were daily concerns, often critical, but then there were concerns that came up and blew away. I had to get used to speaking up on his behalf, no matter what his age. I feared that if I let my guard down, everything would wash down the drain.

We all have different parenting styles, and each needs to be respected. I knew a woman, through a church group, whose first child was born with Down syndrome. I immediately went over to her house to visit and exchange stories. I encouraged her to come to the ARC's support group and gave her leads to other people and agencies. A number of years later, I called her just to check in. So unexpectedly and so pointedly, she exploded. "I am not you; I am not Saint Connie! I can't be like you! I don't enjoy this!" I told her that I do not always enjoy it either, and that I was only trying to help, not tell her what to do. "It's too much for me," she said, nearly in tears, and abruptly hung up. I had not realized how I must have come across; by then I had been in the trenches with Jimmy for well over ten years. I never wanted to make it look easy, it was not easy! I was just more seasoned, after having railed against doctors, educators, family members, Cub Scout leaders – you name it. It was not painless or straightforward, and I was not always victorious. Nevertheless, she asked me not to call her again and I respected that. Two years later, looking at Christmas trees at the Cardinal Cushing School, I saw her and asked how she was. "I need to apologize," she said, "the last time we spoke I was really mean." I excused her, saying, "We all have bad days." A few days later she called to explain further. She said that her daughter was very headstrong and simply ran her ragged. The point is, we all have different kids and different needs. I only hope that new parents find their way to support, and fast.

Being a parent meant I had to get beyond thinking that my kids were going to be my best friends. There were many times when my kids did not even like me. I had to nip certain bad behaviors in the bud or they would not outgrow them. Selfishly, I knew those that went uncorrected would make it harder for me. I will listen to my children, but I make the final decision

Being a parent to Jimmy also means that there are times of sadness. Kevin has a wife who loves him, a beautiful family, a home and a good job. He is building a life and a future for himself, and the same is true for Brendan. I have this chronic sorrow knowing that this will never happen for Jimmy. Maybe I am sad for me; it is a joy to watch your kids build dreams and succeed. Jimmy will not ever be independent, and he does not have big aspirations for the future. His greatest wish each year is for a trip to Indiana to see my cousin, Dr. Jim.

You never know when or what will hit you. I was helping Jimmy shave this morning and noticed grey in his beard. For a few fleeting moments there was tremendous sorrow in simply shaving away those grey stubbles. All I could think of was, here he is, my Jimmy, getting to be an old man. Have I given him enough? Has he enjoyed his life enough? Is there enough? Is there something he does not have that I do not know about? Something else I could do? I sighed and said, "Ohhh

Jimmy, grey hairs!" Jimmy being Jimmy simply laughed and said he liked getting old.

Having a child with special needs means there are not answers right away, if ever. Many years after the Ernie era, I learned from the woman who had rolled up her car window when I went to ask her for help that she had been in the midst of a divorce and did not have the time or the energy to deal with her son's school placement. She was relieved and content knowing that her son had a place to go five days a week; he was safe and happy. She could go to work knowing she had a *babysitter* every day. She went on to say that she did not expect any more than that, and admitted that she never had high expectations for him. She did not think *he* expected or needed any more than that.

When I look back, I realize I was driven. In the beginning I was searching – I did not know what was out there for Jimmy. When programs and services were lacking, I would create what Jimmy needed. Somebody had to. Fortunately, I found other moms who also had fire in their bellies, but I do not expect that same drive from everyone I meet. More often, parents simply do not know what to do and/or they do not have the resources to do it. My sense of purpose and my drive came when two forces aligned in a pivotal, spiritual moment. The first force was really an epiphany. In the hospital, after the shock of Jimmy's diagnosis wore off, I experienced a sacred moment, a moment of falling in love with my Down syndrome baby. The second force, perhaps a natural occurrence after the "falling in love" phenomenon, was the realization that this was going to require putting Jimmy's needs ahead of mine – always.

Periodically, I poke into his life to ask him what he is thinking about, and each time I happily discover that he is so content with his life. When you love someone with special needs, you sometimes wonder whether they know they are different. I get that question a lot; even his brothers ask me if Jimmy knows he has special needs. I have asked him repeatedly in the past. "Are you different than other people, Jimmy?" Sometimes he just looks at me and laughs. I give him examples, such as, "Your brothers drive a car; do you want to drive a car?" Sometimes he will say, "No," and sometimes, "Yeah, why not?" But sometimes I will say, "Okay, I am going to give you the car keys and you can drive us home tonight," to which he answers, "What, are you crazy?"

I recently asked him what it feels like to be an uncle, to live with his mom and not have his own place. It is clear he does not seem to feel any loss or void. I think he perceives a difference, but it does not bother him; it is like me having brown eyes and someone else having blue.

I asked him one time, "Do you want to get married?" and he said, "No." Then I asked, "Do you want to be a father?" He hurriedly answered with a strong "No!" I think he knows his limits and likes to stay in his comfort zone. He does not like to be in a situation where he does not know what to do. I think he is very smart and realizes he would not know how to handle a lot of things.

He loves being a brother, a brother-in-law, a son, and now an uncle. He is fine in the body he has been given, the day he has in front of him, the things presented to him and the people who are in his life. His needs are minimal – just give him kind words, gestures of love and maybe a Red Sox game on TV.

Speaking of sports, the Challengers league existed for 14 years, until Jim died. Patty had also died, so Gerry did not come around, which meant the buddies from the All Stars had gone, too. I kept the league going another two years, trying to coach the two teams and, at the same time, recruit new volunteers. I even coached and ran the bases with the athletes one year with a cast on my foot. It all eventually fell apart. One Challenger still sees me every week and tries to encourage me to start it up again. "I still have my shirt," he says.

Raising someone with special needs is not meant to be a competition; you can only do the best you can with the child you are given. I found that I had to take the time to discover the delight in any given moment. I also had to learn to see the accomplishment from simple interactions – that is the point, isn't it? If you put the time in, you will find the joy. You also have to have humor, and know that when you fail, it is okay. You cannot separate the pleasure, the fun and funniness of being a mom from the full-time job that it is. Jimmy, Brendan and Kevin still make me laugh every day.

Ann, Jane, Connie, Lisa, and Hazel

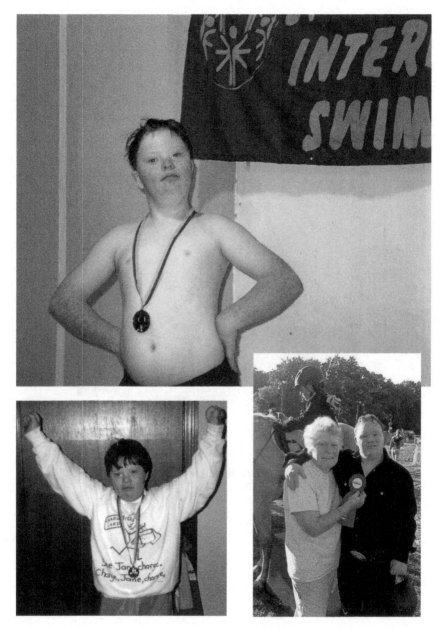

Top: Swimming champ. Above: Young gold medalist Right: Hazel and Edward.

Left: Riding the bus on the first day of school

Below: High School graduation with brothers Kevin and Brendan

Jimmy and Connie

Right: Wendy and Dawn with
their sisters Beth and Sarah

Below: Paula holding Wendy,
with Dawn by her side

The family ready for winter fun: Lisa, Harry, Dawn, Wendy, Sarah and Beth

FIVE COURAGEOUS MOTHERS | Raising Children with Down Syndrome

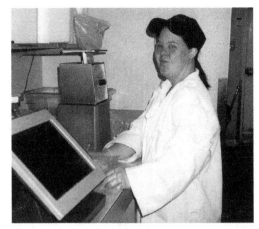

Top Left: Meghan in elementary school

Above: Working at a restaurant

Left: Ann and Meghan

Right: Working in a warehouse

Below: Gold medalist at Special Olympics.

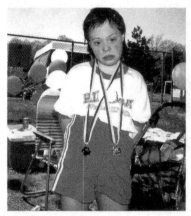

Justin, Derrick and Jane

Chapter Three

Lisa and Harry, Dawn and Wendy

To understand Harry's and my story, you need to know about Paula, Harry's sister.

Paula

Paula was a smart, loving and generous woman. She excelled in school and had plenty of friends but longed to escape her home dominated by an alcoholic father. At the age of 20, she married her boyfriend, Larry.

Paula always wanted children and was ecstatic when, after five years of marriage, she finally conceived. Her pregnancy was typical, so when she gave birth in December 1972 she was not prepared to hear that her baby girl had Down syndrome.

While in the hospital, Paula got advice from doctors, nurses, friends, and family telling her that she should not bring the baby home. "Sending this baby to an institution is the best thing to do," they advised. Her husband, in utter disbelief, agreed, adding, "I can't believe *that thing* was growing inside you."

Paula had already fallen in love with her baby and named her Dawn. The advice was too late; she took Dawn home. While Larry grew to love Dawn, he could not deal with her developmental delays. Paula's marriage began to fall apart, and they soon separated.

She and Dawn began a life together. Fortunately, unlike other babies with Down syndrome, Dawn had no health issues. Paula, eager to know all she could about Down syndrome, researched and found a doctor in Washington, DC, who was conducting a study on the benefits of giving children with Down syndrome high doses of daily vitamins to improve cognition. Paula and Dawn lived in Maryland at the time, so the trip to DC was manageable. They participated in the study, but years later the doctor's vitamin-therapy theory was debunked.

Paula read about potential physical problems for children with Down syndrome, such as poor muscle tone and slow motor development, and became determined to do whatever she could to beat the odds. She had Dawn swimming as an infant and dancing as soon as she could walk. Paula learned that children with Down syndrome have a tendency for language delays and reading difficulties, so she worked tirelessly and taught Dawn to read by the time she was three, long before Dawn's spoken language developed. Informed and resolute, Paula never tired of the daily challenges of Dawn's physical, mental, emotional and social needs.

Paula, a whiz in math, became a full-time computer operator in the early seventies – the days when a computer took up an entire room. She placed Dawn in a preschool program and hired babysitters when necessary. Larry would take Dawn occasionally, but it bothered him that Dawn, now five years old, still wasn't toilet trained. Paula began to notice that Larry was keeping company with some unsavory characters and that his temperament was changing; his moods were erratic and agitated and he seemed depressed. Paula's insights were correct. Three days before Dawn's sixth birthday, Larry killed himself – asphyxiation by carbon monoxide.

Shock hit Paula and Dawn did not understand what it meant. Paula's family back in Massachusetts rallied and over the course of the next year encouraged her to move home so they could help with Dawn.

Paula needed the help. Dawn had a stubborn streak from the moment you can identify one. She was a cute little girl, but if you wanted her to do something she did not want to do she would have a full-on fit. Her extra weight made lifting her difficult.

Dawn was also smart. Early on she learned how to manipulate people and situations to get what she wanted. Often, she'd simply plop herself on the floor, which she knew made lifting her impossible. Given what she wanted, she would get up. Paula, often forced into battles of the wills, was determined to break this recalcitrant streak.

Back in Massachusetts, Paula bought a house in a nice neighborhood with great neighbors. Once, when Dawn was a teenager, Paula was in a rush to leave the house to get an errand done. Dawn was taking her time getting ready – a "skill" she used whenever she did not want to go somewhere. Not falling for this ploy, Paula asked her neighbor to keep an eye out while she ran her errand without Dawn. The neighbor later told Paula that just after she drove away, Dawn ran outside and stood in the yard, looking down the street incredulously. After that, whenever Paula told Dawn they were leaving, Dawn listened.

Paula's mom and dad – he now sober – did help. They would get Dawn onto the school van every morning, prepared for the inevitable race around the van when Dawn did not want to get on.

Paula remained a tireless advocate for Dawn, even getting herself appointed to the Board of the local ARC (Association for Retarded Citizens.) She was rather soft spoken, however, so when an IEP meeting came up she would ask someone from the DPH (Department of Public Health) to accompany her to help her request services she knew Dawn needed. Paula continued the activities she had begun for Dawn in Maryland, signing her up for dance and swimming classes. On top of that, through Special Olympics, Dawn swam twice a week and played basketball at the local school.

Adopting Wendy

When Dawn was ten, Paula adopted Wendy, a five-month-old with Down syndrome. Paula had wanted to expand her family and requested a baby girl with Down syndrome, saying, "that's all I know how to raise." Wendy was a perfect addition. Her agreeable disposition was the cure for Dawn's sometimes obstinate behavior. Paula took a few months off from work to acclimate the family to Wendy and to involve her in early intervention. As time went on, Paula broadened Wendy's life by getting her involved in Special Olympic sports – and modeling. She was a natural! By the time Wendy was five, she was also ice skating. With the help of a private coach, Wendy became an excellent skater, competing against "regular" kids.

The Blending of Families Begins

One of Paula's trusted neighbors babysat for her girls for a few hours when they came home from school. However, in 1994, that neighbor and her family moved to New Hampshire. Between babysitters, Paula asked if we would watch Wendy in the afternoon, since we lived nearby. (Dawn was now old enough to be left alone for a bit without getting into too much trouble.)

At this time, Harry and I had been married for ten years but had only recently started a family. We were blessed with two little girls: Sarah (two) and Elizabeth (one). I was a nurse working per diem around my husband's firefighter schedule so that one of us was always home. It was therefore no problem to welcome Wendy into our home those afternoons. She's sweet by nature and loves little children, so she always looked forward to playing with our girls. One day, while talking with Paula in the kitchen, I heard a muffled cry, "Mommmmmy." I went to the den and started looking around for Sarah. All I found was Wendy sitting on an upside-down toy bucket watching TV, but quickly realized just where Sarah was. I lifted Wendy up, got Sarah out from underneath, and sent Harry down to the cellar to drill holes in the bottom of the bucket.

So, this is how we began to get to know Wendy. We knew Dawn mostly from the many stories about her we had heard over the years. By now, Dawn attended a daily workshop and was doing relatively well. However, as Dawn matured she began to have eating issues. Paula had to avoid bringing certain foods into their house because Dawn would devour them whenever she was home alone. One time, Dawn ate an entire container of Cool Whip and put the empty container back in the fridge. Dawn was obsessed with soda, so Paula would have to keep it away from her by storing it in the trunk of her car in the garage.

Wendy continued to spend afternoons with us, but things were about to change. The following spring, in 1996, Paula, 48, was diagnosed with ovarian cancer and the prognosis was not good. Bravely, she went through surgery and chemotherapy and kept a positive outlook. As a mother of my own two girls, my sadness for Paula was great. My sadness was also infused with guilt – I was glad it was not me.

By December that same year, Paula signed up for home hospice care but continued to work. To this day, I remember hearing Paula tell the hospice nurse that she was a "DNR" (Do Not Resuscitate). Paula had to explain to *me*, the nurse in the family, why that made sense. By then Paula was so weak and emaciated.

Dawn, now 24, knew Paula was sick but she could not help but hold on to her stubborn streak. This was especially true when it came time to shower, which Dawn rebelled against. There were times when Paula and Dawn would wrestle in the hallway, with Paula trying to drag Dawn to the bathroom. On the other hand, Wendy, 13, was oblivious to what was happening to her mom. In late December, after witnessing these difficulties, Harry and I decided that all of them – Paula, Dawn and Wendy – should come to live with us in our little cape.

Paula died on January 7, 1997, at 9:40 pm. When Dawn and Wendy were going to bed that night, we told them that we thought Paula was "going to heaven soon." The next morning, as soon as they got out of bed, we explained that their mom was gone and that they would be staying home with us that day. Dawn pointed to the empty bed and promptly said to Wendy, "See, she's gone. I'm going to work." And, off she went. Dawn likes her routine

Both girls went to the funeral home and saw their mother in an open casket. Wendy did not cry or show any sorrow about her mother's death, but we have learned that this is just how Wendy is. (Years later, my father came to live with us and after nearly two years, he passed. Again, there were no tears from Wendy, no questions about his where-abouts.) While Wendy might not understand death, Dawn, as Paula used to say, takes her cues from those around her. If people are crying, Dawn cries. If they are not, she does not. That is how the wake and funeral went. Many people there cried of course, including Dawn.

Blending

Harry and I knew that Paula's death meant we would become guardians of Dawn and Wendy and we would all be living together. We never thought twice about it; there were no other siblings to step forward. We both knew that is what God expected of us. Aren't we called to "care for the orphaned"?

The day of Paula's funeral it snowed – one of only two snow days we had in 1997. After the bereavement meal we went home, but I wanted to do something fun with the kids, so we went sledding. Just the four girls and me. Sarah and Beth were now three and four; Dawn and Wendy were 24 and 13. Once there, I noticed how crowded it was but went ahead and matched up Dawn with Beth and Wendy with Sarah. I sent Wendy and Sarah down the hill without thinking they needed explicit instructions. As I watched from the top of the hill, I noticed the 13-year-old Wendy talking with the three-year-old Sarah at the bottom. I then saw the decision that they made. Wendy started dragging the sled, with Sarah lying on it, back up the middle of the hill just as a boy flew down the hill, running right over my little girl's face! The boy's parents and I went scrambling down. Fortunately, snow works great on reducing swelling and there was minimal bleeding.

Our new life without Paula begins. The house was too small for us now. Dawn and Wendy, used to their own room, now had to share one with bunk beds. In the middle of the night, you could hear Dawn growling at Wendy for snoring.

I still had a lot to learn. One day, I took the four girls grocery shopping. Before life with Dawn and Wendy, I would put Sarah in the basket of the shopping cart and Beth in the seat. No problem. For some reason, I decided it would be best to use two shopping carts for this first outing with all the girls. I could push one cart with Sarah in the seat and let Wendy push the other with Beth in the seat. Beth would reach out toward Wendy and Wendy would push the cart, let go of it, rush to catch up with it, and then push it several feet ahead of her again. I watched as Wendy pushed the cart away for the third time and Beth tried to reach for Wendy. Beth flipped right out of the carriage onto the unforgiving grocery store floor. "What is going on here?" I said to myself. "I'm going to get my own kids killed if I don't anticipate better." I quickly reached for a bag of frozen peas, which also reduce swelling.

We started looking for a new place for our larger family. One day Harry and I were out with just Sarah and Beth to look at a lot in a nearby town. A man who lived in the house next to the lot was outside, so we chatted with him. He was drawn to our adorable little girls and seemed to like us. We mentioned that we also had two other girls in the family. "both with Down syndrome." His next words were, "You know, they're building off of Auburn Street, too." Hmmm. Harry and I awkwardly packed the girls in the car and drove away in silence. Minutes later, I asked Harry, "Do you think we will get discriminated against because we have kids with special needs now?" His response was immediate. "Why? Because that guy is telling us where else to build?" I suspected this man also held other prejudices, so there was some satisfaction learning later that a gay couple built next door to him.

Life with Dawn

We ended up building in a wonderful neighborhood. Dawn and Wendy had their rooms again and life moved along. However, six months after Paula died, Dawn started showing some bizarre behaviors. First, she claimed that a bee had flown in her ear and she could not get it out. She could still hear it buzzing. Still more worrisome was that Dawn's usual voracious appetite suddenly ceased; she simply wouldn't eat. Not knowing what was going on and thinking she was being obstinate, I insisted she eat. She would sit in front of a piece of pizza, take a tiny bite and then sneak it out of her mouth discreetly. I was so busy with the three others that I did not notice how little she was eating. (Little did we know she had also stopped drinking.) One morning, she passed out while waiting for her van to the workshop and was hospitalized. After a multitude of tests, we were told she was dehydrated but had nothing else physically wrong with her. (Later, we learned that Dawn's latent grieving – this six-month marker – is textbook timing for people with Down syndrome to experience grief.)

However, Dawn was insisting that her mother was telling her not to eat. She ended up in a psych hospital and was diagnosed with a psychotic depression. She would not take medication. She would not drink. She pulled IVs out immediately after they were put in. After five weeks of hospitalization Dawn looked awful; she had lost 25 pounds. The attending psychiatrist told Harry and me that ECT (electroconvulsive therapy) held the most hope for her. We were not all that familiar with it and leery, having seen images from "One Flew over the Cuckoo's Nest." When we told him our fears, he replied, "Well, I would not have wanted to get my appendix out 50 years ago either, but that treatment and this one have made great advances." The courts, because Dawn was an adult, appointed a young, fledgling lawyer to be her guardian ad litum. He told the courts ECT was not necessary. We fought his opinion, wondering what he knew about this eating disorder or about people with Down syndrome. We were given a second hearing. Dawn's doctor testified candidly in court. "This young woman is no longer having bowel sounds because she is not eating or drinking, and her colon will die if she doesn't get this ECT treatment." The judge dismissed the guardian ad litum and Dawn underwent the electroconvulsive therapy. Over the next ten days she had five treatments. Soon, we were happy to hear, she was getting into trouble for going into other patient's rooms and stealing food and soda.

After Dawn was physically stabilized, she was admitted to another hospital for psychiatric help. There, Dawn was diagnosed as bipolar with a schizophrenic component. Hospital clinicians helped her understand that her mom was dead, she was not coming back and there was nothing anyone could do to make it different. Dawn remained in a deep state of grieving.

This weeks-long episode was emotional and scary for us all. Dawn was not eating, drinking or listening to her beloved music. It was as if she was shriveling up in front of us. We realized that she probably struggled with mental illness even while her mother was alive, and never got treated for it.

Soon, it seemed that Dawn was healed. Or so the hospital thought. They discharged her but when I went to pick her up she said she was not ready to leave. She wanted "to live there." Why not? I thought. This was a perfect life for Dawn – not much was expected of her and she was given food and snacks. Despite Dawn insisting that she did not want to go home, the doctor and staff came out to help get her into the car. She said she was worried that her mother's ghost was still in the house. Nervously, I started driving home when suddenly she opened the car door to get out. Still driving 35 miles per hour, I grabbed her arm to keep her from falling out and inadvertently turned the steering wheel. All I could see were the headlights of an oncoming car, driving straight at us. At the last second, I turned the wheel back and pulled into a driveway. I cried and screamed, "You almost killed us. If you don't want to come home, that's fine! I've got three other kids who need me, so stay put and I will bring you back to the hospital!" I turned around and drove right back. Dawn got out of the car with a familiar victory spring in her step while I tearfully recounted to the staff what happened. I told them that I was not going to bring her home until she was ready.

When the time came to bring her home, we needed a plan to get Dawn to come into the house. I enlisted a friend to pick her up and told Dawn she would be staying with her for a while. That seemed to work. Dawn agreed to come back into our house only to pick up her cherished CD collection. Once Dawn was in the house, our friend quickly left. Dawn gathered her CDs and went to the door to go. When she saw that our friend had gone, Harry said, "She left Dawn. You'll stay with us, okay?" Dawn turned around, went back to her room and started listening to her CDs, never mentioning her mother's ghost again. Dawn was taking antidepressants at the time, but some of her issues were behavioral.

We were told to find outside clinicians and schedule follow-up appointments for Dawn. These appointments were never easy. The new clinicians did not seem to fully understand Down syndrome, which made communication difficult. The first thing they would ask Dawn is how she was. She would say, "fine," which is the only answer she knows to this question. Little else was forthcoming.

With Dawn back home we began again, readjusting not only to life in our new home but to all the events that had taken place. Dawn continued to go to her workshop, and Wendy to school. However, slowly we became more aware of Dawn's persistent sneaky side. We used to keep change in a kitchen drawer, and Dawn was allowed to count out 65 cents each night to buy a soda the next day. One night, shortly before a trip we were taking to Disneyworld, I happened to put ten one-hundred-dollar bills – our vacation spending money – in that drawer. The next day, Dawn's workshop called to say that someone saw her put a one-hundred-dollar bill in the vending machine to get an extra soda. Thank goodness the machine did not take it! Dawn thought she was good at being sneaky, but, fortunately, she was usually found out.

We knew that Dawn was obsessed with CDs, lotions and pens, but soon we noticed that she was hoarding them. We asked a behaviorist to help us deal with some of these difficult behaviors. He encouraged us to begin a positive reinforcement reward system. Dawn would earn a smiley face for a day of good behavior, and after earning a certain number of smiley faces, she was allowed to get a new CD. It seemed to work. Eventually we had to buy a couple of CD towers for her to hold them all. However, even with at least 80 CDs, Dawn would sneak into Wendy's room and take some of hers. In fact, if she saw any laying around the house she would grab them and write her name on the cases with a sharpie she scoffed from the kitchen pencil cup. Then she would hurriedly shove them in the already full CD towers until the case, and sometimes the CD, broke. If you reprimanded her she had no shame; she would begin talking to herself as if in a two-way conversation. "Dawn?" "What?" "Is Lisa being rude to you?" "Yes." "Well, don't listen to her!" Sarah and Beth came to think this monologue-dialog of hers was entertaining.

Life with Wendy

Wendy continued at her great middle school program, part of the North River Collaborative. Unlike Dawn, Wendy had trouble learning to read more than a few words. One summer we hired a tutor, but she did not get too far. She was able to learn emergency words like "exit" and, as she would say, "high voltrage."

When it was time for Wendy to attend high school, we enrolled her in the regional school. We did not realize, however, that they did not have a special needs class. After the first day, she came home, went right to the study and pulled out an encyclopedia (marked A-D), telling us that she needed to do a book report on *insects*. She did not have a clue as to what was going on in the mainstreaming classes. I did not hesitate and went to the school to tell them that I wanted her in a class that would work on her ADLs (Activity of Daily Living Skills). I wanted her to be able to tie her own shoes and cut her own food. Soon, they started "Homeroom 129" for kids with special needs. After a while, the wonderful teacher realized how much all the kids liked to cook and eat and established "Café 129." Staff, students, and family could come and buy lunch every Tuesday. Wendy enjoyed her high school days and went to her prom with a group of classmates.

Family Life

Despite the age discrepancies, life with the four girls was fun, most of the time. Holidays and birthdays were big deals and we made them festive. Whenever a new calendar came out, Dawn and Wendy would scour it to find what day of the week their birthday was going to be on and remind us over and over. Christmas, of course, was always huge. In an attempt to help Wendy and Dawn "mature" I reiterated what their mother Paula had told them, "There is no Santa Claus." While they might not have liked that news (Wendy still thinks there is a Santa Claus), I thought it was important for them to understand – until my insistence boomeranged. One night, talking about Christmas lists at the dinner table with Sarah (five) and Beth (six), Dawn announced, "So, I know my mom already told me *she* was Santa Claus, you don't have to pretend." Silence. Harry and I looked at each other, then over to Sarah and Beth. "Oh Dawn!" I said quickly. "You are so funny!

Paula *felt* like Santa Claus because she liked to give presents." Here I am now trying to talk Dawn back into believing in Santa, which we did. Poor girl. She must have been so confused. Another Christmas, Dawn was discussing presents with one of her cousins. They reminded her that it is better to give than to receive. Dawn quickly responded, "Yeah, so what are you going to give me?"

Since her hospitalization, Dawn has been taking an antidepressant, but even with the medication she can be difficult. We were big on exercise and wanted both Dawn and Wendy to walk the one-mile loop around our neighborhood when they got home from their respective day programs. It was a safe walk and could be done wearing headphones, listening to their favorite music. Dawn started objecting, saying she wanted to "sit around," but I insisted. She would eventually go, but once outside she would cross the street and start yelling, pointing her finger at the house, scolding Harry or me. After she was done screaming at us she would slowly walk the loop, singing out loud to her CDs. A neighbor told us he was drawn outside by Dawn's voice, thinking it was the sound of an animal being hit by a car.

Like any siblings, the four of them irritated each other at different times. Sarah was in the kitchen once when Dawn was getting herself breakfast. I heard Sarah's bellow from another room. "Mommmm, Dawn just sneezed into the box of Cocoa Krispies!" I said, "Well, tell her it is *her* box now." Another time, on a car ride, Sarah cried out, "Mom, Dawn just wiped a worm on my leg!" "What? Where did the worm come from?" "Her leg!" she answered. I would often tell Sarah and Beth, "You know, you don't have to get *me* involved in every issue. Someday, you two could be in charge of Dawn and Wendy." From another room I hear Beth yell out, "I get Wendy!"

Dawn and Wendy were both relatively healthy physically, but every now and then one would say, "I pulled a muscle in my head." I have no idea what that meant, but assumed it was a headache. Tylenol worked. (A percentage of people with Down syndrome have Atlanto-axial Instability, which makes one's neck unstable. It was never diagnosed in either of them.)

Once, Dawn had that same complaint, but I noticed she looked like she was going to pass out. Finding her blood pressure low, I called an ambulance. All this happened just before dinner on a night when Sarah and Beth invited a friend to eat with us before their much-anticipated high school talent show. Sarah and Beth recall the night perfectly. The fire department and ambulance crew bolted through the kitchen while they were sitting down to dinner with their friend and then, minutes later, while trying to enjoy their dinner, the crew whizzed by again with Dawn now passed out on a stretcher. All the while, I am trying to tell Sarah, Beth and their friend to hurry up and eat. As it turned out, I went to the hospital with Dawn while Harry took the poor girls to school. Dawn was fine.

The summer of 2008 was a turning point for us with Dawn. Her behavior had become more oppositional; we did not know why, nor could the psychologist offer any insight. She continued taking and hoarding things from everyone in the house. She would get upset when we took our items back or even touched them. She also continued to plop herself on the floor just to be difficult, blocking doorways or staircases. Turmoil ensued.

Around the Fourth of July, we rented a small cottage and bunkhouse on a lake in Maine. That gave us plenty of space, I thought, to hold the six of us as well as my sister, Kathie, and a niece and nephew close to our girls' ages. Harry drove to the lake early in the day with Dawn, Wendy and the four younger kids. After work, my sister picked up our dog and me, and we drove together.

The plan was that my husband, our nephew and some of the kids would sleep in the bunkhouse; my sister and I would luxuriate in the one-bedroom cottage, with any leftover kids on twin beds on a screened-in porch. My husband called me after they arrived to warn me that the bunkhouse was uninhabitable. Not only did it have a sinister looking glow from the only light bulb in the place, it was filthy – with cobwebs galore and bug-infested mattresses. Everyone would have to squeeze into the cottage. We gave Dawn and Wendy the bedroom with the queen-size bed and the rest of us slept on the floor, on top of cushions from the couch and loveseat. With the nine of us and the dog, it was tight. The next morning, we made the best of it and went kayaking on the lake. Dawn, not especially happy, said she could not wait to get home and go back to work. At lunchtime, Harry grilled and we ate outside. Everyone was drinking milk with their lunch, but Dawn said she wanted a soda. "When your milk is gone," Harry said. Dawn looked right at Harry, picked up her glass of milk and poured it on the grass. This was the beginning.

After lunch, most of us went out for a few hours to explore the town. When we returned I checked in on Dawn, who was lying on the bed looking at magazines. I glanced at the bureau in the bedroom and noticed the empty jewelry holder, shaped like a dress form, which had held a necklace when we arrived. I found the necklace, now broken, in Dawn's bag. She wanted it, took it and broke it. I was so angry and ...so sad.

I also noticed a putrid smell in the room, and asked Dawn if she needed to use the bathroom. "No," she said, "I just did." I insisted she get up and in so doing, saw that she had neglected to wipe herself properly, leaving a mess that seeped through her shorts and onto the bedspread. Dawn refused to shower so I tried to drag her to the bathroom, calling Harry to help. This was the first time in our 11-and-a-half years with Dawn that we had reached our limit; we did not know if we could handle her behavior any longer. My kids still do not like thinking of the state of Maine as a vacation destination.

Moving On

When we got home, Dawn was out of control, so she returned to the psych hospital. She stabilized after several weeks of treatment and medication changes, but we could no longer deal with her behavior issues. We contacted the Department of Developmental Services (DDS) to request a new living situation for her. They were very helpful and agreed to place Dawn with a wonderful woman who had done respite care for us in the past. Like the "Burrow" in the Harry Potter story, the house teemed with activity – with people in and out constantly. It was chaotic at times, but filled with lots of love. Dawn was happy there. Dawn has since moved to another woman's home for adult foster care, because the "Burrow" exceeded the number of allowable children or adults in foster care, according to the state.

That was six years ago. Since then, Dawn has had behavioral issues that have required more hospitalizations and med changes, but she is doing well, and her living situation is a blessing to us all. Her caretaker is extremely patient and supportive. Dawn continues to go to the workshop, and we see her at least once a month, as well as for birthdays and holidays. Harry also continues to pick Dawn up to take her and Wendy bowling.

Wendy has now lived with us for more than 20 years – wearing a sweet smile on her face the whole time. We know her IQ is not as high as her sister's, but she lives happily in her own little world. During dinner table discussions, Wendy listens but does not know what we are talking about, nor does she care. If you try to engage her or ask what she thinks, she is apt to say something silly like, "Mark Jerony loves ketchup." Or, "The king of pop made lunch with me today in the kitchen." She continues in her day program and Harry, now retired, still wakes to make sure she is ready for the van and appropriately dressed. Without Harry's guidance, Wendy comes out wearing winter clothes in the summer and the reverse in the winter.

I am planning to retire soon, and Harry and I know it is time to help Wendy live independently from us. DDS has found a very active, interesting home with others with special needs. We tried to prepare Wendy for this move by talking every night at dinner about this great house, with fun things to do. We would ask, "Wouldn't it be great if you could live there?" She would sit there smiling and nodding at us, but we sensed that she did not quite get it. One night before she moved, Harry was sitting with her and said, "Wendy, are you going to miss me?" In this one lucid moment, Wendy said, "I'll be fine." She *is* fine. She *is* happy.

Sarah and Beth have also moved out and are enjoying their own lives. Harry and I are now empty nesters. God has been so good to us, that when others ask, "How could you do it?" we wonder, "How could we not?"

Chapter Four

Ann Carroll and Meghan

I did not do anything special. I did for my daughter what anybody would do for their child, but in the beginning, accepting Meghan's Down syndrome was hard, very hard. This was not what I had expected.

The Birth

The day after Meghan's birth, one of the pediatricians in the practice, Dr. Spitz, came into my room saying, "I suspect your baby has Down syndrome." The air was knocked out of me. I was dumbfounded. Because I had very little exposure to people with Down syndrome, I immediately thought the worst. My image was of an overweight person with little communication. How can I possibly do this? My next thought was, "She's going to be a woman? How am I going to tell her about her the birds and the bees?"

Dr. Spitz simply walked out of the room leaving me with this news to deal with, without any support. He had no bedside manner and no clue how to handle me. Sad and very confused, I called my mother and my husband, Bob.

My obstetrician, Dr. Penza, came in shortly after that. He sat with me and calmly said, "It's going to be okay and you're going to be okay." Just hearing those words somehow got me through the first hours.

117

My mother arrived quickly. Sitting close, she leaned in and said softly, "Ann, she's beautiful!" That was my first indication that this just might be okay. I began to breathe.

It was January 27, 1981. I was 24 years old and this was my first baby. Meghan's Down syndrome, Standard Trisomy 21*, was simply a fluke and I was not at all prepared.

A girlfriend came in to see me, but only one. I surmised people were staying away because they did not know what to say. I was mourning the loss of that perfect baby I spent nine months expecting. My hospital room was overflowing with flowers instead of the gifts you would normally receive after the birth of a child.

On day three or four, a woman named Connie came to my room. The hospital had asked her to come in and speak to new mothers who had given birth to a child with special needs. Connie first consoled me and then tried to educate me about Down syndrome. She opened a photo album of her son who, too, had Down syndrome. Listless, I began flipping through the pages and landed on a picture of him in a Halloween costume. Only then did it register. We are going to be okay. My daughter *might* be able to go trick or treating. The horrendous image I had of Down syndrome did not allow me to think that she would be able to do anything. Remembering my mother's comforting words and seeing this boy in a Halloween costume were teeny inklings of hope.

---

*Standard Trisomy 21 is when the extra chromosome 21 comes from either the egg or sperm cell. Between 90% and 95% of all Down syndrome is Standard Trisomy 21. (There are three different types of Down syndrome: Standard Trisomy 21, Translocation, and Mosaicism. Translocation is caused when a piece of chromosome 21 is located on another chromosome such as chromosome 14. The person with Translocation Trisomy 21 will have 46 chromosomes but will have the genetic material of 47 chromosomes. The person with Translocation Trisomy 21 will exhibit all the same characteristics of a person with Standard Trisomy 21 since they have three copies of chromosome 21. Translocation occurs between 3% and 5% of cases of Down syndrome. Mosaicism is when a person has a mix of cells, some containing 46 chromosomes and some containing 47 chromosomes. Mosaicism occurs in 2% to 5% of cases of Down syndrome. A person with Mosaic Down syndrome may exhibit all, some, or none of the characteristics of Down syndrome depending on the percent of cells carrying the extra chromosome and where these cells are located. The vast majority of cases of Down syndrome are not inherited. Only in cases of Translocation Down syndrome and then in only 1 of 3 cases of this type of Down syndrome is the condition inherited. These inherited cases occur because one of the parents is a carrier.)

After several days in the hospital, we loaded the flowers into the car to go home. It dawned on me that nobody had sent a present for Meghan, except my mom; she knew. Friends or family probably did not know what to say or give. Flowers spoke volumes of their sympathy. It was soon after that I realized my friends and family went through the same confusion and feelings I had. They did what they thought was right and soon we started to receive lovely, thoughtful gifts for our new baby girl.

My pediatrician suggested I take Meghan into Tufts Medical Center in Boston where they could "follow her." There wasn't anything wrong with her; her heart was strong and she was physically fit. I now realize that they wanted to make sure that she was thriving, fearful of what I was experiencing. Tufts doctors were on a mission to make sure that we, as a family, would do well and care for her.

Support: Individuals, Groups and Programs

Acceptance of Meghan's Down syndrome was gradual. It helped to have people visit, and my husband, Bob, gave me enormous emotional support. "It's gonna be okay, Ann," he'd say. "We're going to be a family. We'll get through this." He was my rock. However, just as *I* was turning the corner towards acceptance, he started to fall apart. This shift in his stability was a bit scary, but I realized it was his turn to go through the same doubt and despair I had experienced. Luckily, he was honest with me and thankfully I, a bit stronger by then, was able to offer him a listening ear. I do not think anyone who gives birth unexpectedly to a child with Down syndrome can say that all is going to be fine and mean it. We both had to endure a period when it was okay not to be okay. The process of my acceptance might not have been an extremely *long* time, but it was a very intense time.

I do not know exactly at what point things turned around, but eventually the reality of the fact that Meghan has Down syndrome was okay. I started to do some research and found an occupational therapist, Mary, in a neighboring town. Her first words endeared me to her instantly. "Ann," she said, "people are going to tell you that 'God chose you because you're a good mother.' You are going to get all sorts of prayers and you're going to be praised to the max." Then she looked me straight in the eyes and said, "You know what? This has nothing to do with being a good mother. It's a bad roll of the dice." She was so-

berly honest and her words were such a relief. I had already been thinking that God *would not* have chosen me! He would have picked someone much, much stronger.

According to Mary, Meghan had exceptionally low muscle tone.
Mary taught me several, common sense interventions. For example,
she told me to always carry Meghan with her legs held firmly together.
This, she said, would ward off the typical wide gate characteristic of
people with Down syndrome. She also told me to use cloth diapers.
With cloth I could twist the diaper tighter, leaving less bulk between
her legs, which would keep her from spreading her hips. And, with
Meghan not even a month old, Mary had me put her on a medicine ball
and roll her back and forth, forcing Meghan to use her stomach muscles. All the seemingly little things Mary told me in the beginning made
huge differences, seen in Meghan's physical appearance and stride today.

Like any new mom, my early days and months with Meghan were
confusing. Everything was a question. To make it more difficult, I did
not know if half the things she did was because she was a newborn, or
because she had Down syndrome. I remember calling my neighbor, a
nurse, when Meghan's face would turn beat red. "Kathy," I said pan-
icking, "can you come over please?" When I told her why, she told me
calmly that Meghan was simply having a bowel movement.

Alarmed on another occasion, I listed all my fears to the doctor.
"Meghan doesn't wake up enough! She doesn't eat enough! She sleeps
eight hours!" "She'll be okay, Ann. She's fine," he would say. If she
was my second child this might have been easier, but everything she
did or didn't do was such an uncertainty.

I was lucky to have a great mother and father around for support,
as well as six close siblings. My father would come to my house each
morning to wait for his ride to work. We would have coffee together.
Meghan would toddle over to him and indicate she wanted a sip. He
happily obliged and waited for his mug to be returned. Despite the
backwash, he would drink the rest of the coffee without thinking twice.
I smiled, thinking, "Oh my God, he must love her!" Meghan was three
when my father died, but my mother was a steady presence until she
died in 2000, almost 20 years later. All of my siblings have been fabulous, but perhaps my sisters Mary and Jean, who lived nearby, were the
most supportive. Mary has a heart as big as they come and always says

the right things. Jean is my and Meghan's go-to person. She will do anything for me – anything – and she has.

Connie left her phone number when she visited at the hospital and I used it frequently. She was especially helpful in Meghan's early days; it was from Connie that I began to understand what to expect. I learned that, oddly enough, Dr. Penza had delivered four babies with Down syndrome all within a very short period. I found their names and phone numbers. All of us new moms – Kathy, Pam, Cheryl, Connie, Maureen and I – would get together once a month when our children were two or three. We shared suggestions on things we could do to make this new life a little easier. We also shared our stories of the day we learned that our babies had Down syndrome. None of us had a positive experience. Together, we discussed how our doctors could have made the experience better simply by using different words and adopting more positive demeanors. We decided we could help change this and set about talking to pediatricians about different ways to approach new mothers (and dads) who had delivered babies born with Down syndrome. We made sure that doctors had our phone numbers and we asked to be called into the hospital to visit any new parent of a baby born with Down syndrome. By then, we had a box of tools to share with them.

I got pregnant with my son, Robert, immediately after I had Meghan. They are 14 months apart. I requested an amniocentesis, a procedure that was brand new in 1983. The day it was scheduled, the doctor at the hospital looked at me askance and, seeing I was young, asked, "Why are *you* having this?" I was angry; he had no business questioning my decision.

I had the amnio and an ultrasound, and everything came back just fine. However, it did not matter; I was convinced my baby was going to have CP (Cerebral Palsy). Here I was doing these tests to alleviate worry, but I was still sure this next baby was going to be disabled. I believe now that I spent so much time at the Floating Hospital and was exposed to so many disabilities it was hard to see beyond them. That is how I was thinking then.

Robert was born free of any disability. Having him was the best thing I could have done. I probably did not think so at the time because I was so busy, but it was absolutely the greatest stimulation for Meghan and she was companionship for Rob. For me, it was like having twins. Rob, of course, wasn't walking and Meghan did not walk until after she was two; I carried one on each hip. I was not one to sit around; wherever I went, those two came with me. It is "full on" when you have two little ones.

I can remember walking through the mall with Robert in a carriage. People would stop me all the time and say, "Oh, he's *so* cute!!" I did not get that when I strolled with Meghan – nobody commented. I would not have seen this firsthand had Robert not come along so quickly. I so hope this has changed – people probably did not know what to say.

My support group continued to be an important center of my life. It was here that we would compare stories and ask questions, one of which was trying to figure out how Down syndrome happened. What was our common denominator? I began with questions such as, "Did you pump your own gas?" That was ruled out. "Did your dog have fleas when you were pregnant?" "No." We continued to wonder and decided to separately review the nine months before our child's delivery, but each theory we came up with only ended up sounding preposterous, sending us into fits of laughter. Humor united us and saved us. We were stymied, though; the "why" of it all was always on our minds. Our tight group allowed us to say things to each other, things only *we* could share. Eventually, the husbands of this group became friendly and we began having dinners at each other's homes, frequently.

We continued to learn from each other and together sought out the next step for our children, which turned out to be the Kennedy-Donovan Center. Each morning, we would participate in their group sing-alongs, their strengthening exercises, and other therapy-type activities. Mary, the head of the center, was in charge for a reason. She was extremely positive and had much experience. Each child in her group was loved and cared for, but not one was treated differently than any child anywhere. She was a major support for me, in particular. I remember thinking that if I had a question, as insignificant as it might seem, I could simply go to Mary. She ingratiated herself into our group and we welcomed her to all our social gatherings. She did not have a family member or an offspring with Down syndrome, but somehow she found her niche with this population and was just plain good at it.

To alleviate some of the frustration with our children's poor speech, some of us used sign language, which was taught at the Kennedy Center. We learned simple signing for words often used, such as cookie, juice or drink. My family also learned some of the basic signs.

Like me, they were happy to find a way to communicate with Meghan and alleviate some of her frustration. None of us ever signed without also saying the word and asking Meghan to repeat it. Eventually, she became more verbal.

From the Kennedy Center, Meghan went to the North River Collaborative's ECC (Early Childhood Center). She continued to sign but as she began to develop more language, signing was discontinued. Meghan was fortunate enough to have Cindy and Jean and several other top-notch teachers in this ECC program. They worked hard and knew what they were doing. Language Arts was a process and these teachers persevered. Every day, Jean would read a page from the book, "Sarah on the Prairie," and the whole class would read it aloud in anticipation of being able to act it out. It was from persistent reading, speaking and acting that it clicked. Meghan, one day, came home reading.

Changes in My Family

In 1986, when Meghan was five, Bob and I had a new baby girl, Kathryn. We were a complete family then and from the get-go the three kids were wonderful with each other. Everywhere I went with Meghan, Rob and Kathryn came. That meant not only tagging along to my support group, but to Meghan's classrooms and other activities. Rob and Kathryn did nothing but benefit from this. Compassion became part of their DNA.

Bob and I, however, were not getting along well. I knew he suffered from something even when we married, but this *something* worsened over time. I could never predict what any day would bring and always wondered what his mood would be when he came home. He was never abusive or physical, but he was distant. He would often pull in the driveway, go upstairs, and fall asleep. We went to marriage counseling but it did not help. Unfortunately, I took on his moodiness and constantly wondered what I was doing to bring this on. I worked endlessly to make everything perfect. Eventually, Bob and I were the ones who figured it out and finally got him to the right doctor. He was suffering from undiagnosed clinical depression, something people were not as aware of then. He started taking medication but by then it was too late. I had lost all feeling for him.

I stayed married by creating my own happy, little life. This separate life began by going to family functions without Bob, who did not want to go anyway. I was not one to go out much socially, so my world shrunk to include me, the kids and my big family. My mom had a house on a pond in Pembroke where we all spent many wonderful hours with lots of cousins and family members. Meghan's grandmother took a special interest in her. It became obvious to the cousins that my mom did *anything* Meghan asked, so they quickly learned to persuade Meghan to get things for them. "Hey Meghan, go ask Grandmother if you can get McDonalds." "Of course, you can get McDonalds," she would say, all because *Meghan* asked. My mom loved each of her grandchildren dearly. I look back and realize just how fortunate I was. How many people do not have a mom around? How many people do not have a family to support them unconditionally? How many families might have excluded Meghan?

When I asked for a divorce, Bob moved out. That was in 1994, over 20 years ago. Kathryn was eight, Rob was 12 and Meghan was 13. Bob was heartbroken. I blamed myself until I finally sought professional help. For a long time after he left I did not know where he was living; he simply skipped town and lost contact with us, his family. He finally reappeared in 2000, when both Rob and Meghan graduated from high school. Then, and now, he has never acknowledged holidays or his children's birthdays. When this realization hits Meghan, it is every bit as painful as it was the day she heard the news of him moving out. You do not know the right thing to do. I remember asking my sister Jean, "Should I send a card and sign it from him, or should I just let it go? Would that make Meghan think more about it? Am I opening up a can of worms?" Her heart aches to this day. She gets so emotional when he is mentioned, or when an important event or holiday comes up, that she will sob to the point of being inconsolable. She knows her father's birthday, but we could not send a card; we had no address. Meghan has a gift of knowing everyone's birthdates. If you do not know someone's, just ask Meghan; she never forgets a birthday.

A short time ago, I found out where Bob lived and picked up the phone to ask him to contact his kids but got no real response. I learned that he is critically ill with emphysema. How do I tell Meghan?

Our lives moved along without him. I wanted Meghan to receive First Holy Communion, so I went to our local parish to sign her up for the required classes. The priest stopped me, saying, "She cannot go through this. We do not have a program for her." I offered to modify the course, do whatever accommodation was needed for her to receive this sacrament. His answer was still a firm, "No." I found another parish, St. Theclas, where she enrolled in religious education classes and made her First Holy Communion without any special requirements. Later in life, Meghan was confirmed at St. Theclas as well.

Being a single parent meant attending a never-ending stream of sports and activities. Meghan and I would never miss going to watch the Mites, Midgets and Peewee games. These were big deal, grammar school football teams in our town. Rob and Kathryn both played football, and out of 64 players on the Mites, Kathryn was the only girl, and every bit as good as any of them. Meghan would go down to the field and cheer Rob on with a bit of her showmanship. Her enthusiasm and sense of rhythm caught the eye of the cheerleading coach, who soon handed her one of their uniforms and asked her to join them. The cheerleading team loved her and encouraged her in all ways. She quickly became their mascot. Meghan's new sense of identity began that year, as did her visibility in this town, where happily she continues to be recognized today.

School Days

All through Meghan's pre-school years, she received the therapy services she needed: speech, occupational and physical. However, as she got older, the therapies dropped in intensity and some disappeared altogether. It was a constant struggle to interject *my* ideas for what she needed. I was steamrolled by officials at every level, telling me that "the programs had already been established" and weren't up for discussion. Often, however, what was in place was not working for Meghan. Despite my inherent nature of not wanting to rock the boat, I knew I had to become vocal to make sure Meghan got the services she needed to help her succeed in life.

Elementary school for this population was held at the Cedar School in a neighboring town. Meghan's biggest obstacle has always been struggling to be understood: I often said that if Meghan's language skills were honed, she would be President. Her speech had improved by the time she entered Cedar School, but to understand her fully, you needed to know the context of what she was talking about – the people, place or incident. I fought for more speech therapy for Meghan, and finally got it. For some reason, I was uneasy about my victory and decided to slip into the classroom to be sure the teachers and therapists were doing what they were supposed to be doing. All it took was one visit for my instinct to be verified. I entered the school, turned a corner and saw Meghan and her speech therapist sitting at a desk outside the classroom, in the hallway. Classes were changing; kids were flooding the corridors and shouting to each other while her therapist leaned on her elbow, holding her hand up to block Meghan's roaming eyes. "Pay attention. Pay attention!" she demanded. How could Meghan sustain eye contact with the barrage of noise and high school students streaming by? Yes, speech therapy was now in her schedule, but I was not told that they did not have a designated, quiet room in which to hold it. I was furious. "If you are expecting Meghan to get anything out of this, you need to find a spot conducive to work and this is not it." They never did end up with an official speech room or office space of their own, but instead carved out a section of the busy classroom for this therapy. To this day, understanding Meghan's speech can be difficult. People who do not know her or don't have a reference point, find her difficult to comprehend. Even I do not get her all the time. She has a propensity to talk fast, so I have to slow her down. Even if I enticed her, I do not think Meghan would ever again step near a speech therapy room. Those days are over.

Academically, Meghan made great strides early on in ECC. She learned to read, tell time on both a digital and analog clock, and was gaining skills in independence. However, a troublesome area for Meghan has been her inability to count money. Meghan knows how much a cheeseburger costs but cannot count out the loose change to pay for it. I was disturbed when I went into the middle school classroom and saw them teaching money with plastic coins that looked and felt nothing like actual money. I ended up bringing in real coins – dimes, nickels, quarters and pennies – saying, "This might be more effective." I was on them all the time and knew her teachers well in both middle and high school. I am not sure what *they* thought, but I bet they became sick of me.

As Meghan continued to mature, she developed into a bit of an imp. I once got a call from one of the teachers who said, "Ann, I want you to know that Meghan said she didn't have any lunch today. She told staff that 'there's no money at home and mom won't have any until Friday. My father gets paid then.' I know this is not the case, but some people will hear this and think that she is coming to school with no lunch. I just wanted to let you know." From an early age Meghan was calculating and knew she could manipulate situations; in this case, she knew she would be offered a different and, in her eyes, a better lunch. Our whole family knew this about her. I got another call from school when Meghan was a bit older. (Keep in mind Rob was in this school with her.) "Nobody saw this," said the teacher who phoned, "but you need to know that Meghan brought in a picture of herself and her siblings naked in the bathtub." Smirking, I thought, Meghan knew *exactly* what she was doing. She loves to embarrass Rob. Another day, driving with the two of them in the car, we saw one of Rob's friends walking home. I asked him if we should pick him up. Rob said, "Sure," but then realized Meghan was in the back seat. He quickly turned around and said sternly, "If you open your mouth, I'm gonna kill you." Normally, I would have spoken to him about his words, but I thought about Meghan's penchant for shaking things up and decided, "I'm going to give you that, one Rob." Meghan needs to hear this.

Another thing she would do when she got into trouble in school was to plead, "Don't call my mother. Please don't call my mother!" She would make me sound like a mean, old ogre just waiting at home to devour her. She is smarter than people understand, and she knows how to play it. Meghan can turn on the waterfalls and unless you figure that out, she will have complete control over you. One supervisor caught on to her and would call her out saying, "Meghan, that's not appropriate now," or "That's not going to work with me. Let's stop that." Strangely enough, Meghan really liked her.

Though she might have been a rascal, I can honestly say that in all of Meghan's school years she experienced bullying only once that I know of. That was from a neighbor who, in front of her young friends, shooed Meghan home, saying, "You can't play with us, nobody understands you anyway." I was concerned about how the kids in her special needs room were perceived and treated by others. At the Cedar School, a group of us started "Disabilities Week." Our intention was to educate the student population through hands-on experiences of varied disabilities. Students, for example, were given gloves to wear all day to see how hard it would be to manage with thick, Down syndrome-like fingers. Another time kids had to wear blindfolds for a day. We mixed it up. Since her experience at this school was positive, I have to think that our goal of sensitizing other students to special needs was achieved.

Maybe it's because of my own image of Down syndrome, but ever since Meghan was young, I have wanted so much to alter and advance people's perceptions of Down syndrome. I once said to my sister-in-law, Linda, "It is so important to me, now that I know about Down syndrome, to educate people about it. I can't tell you how hard I work to keep Meghan clean, neat and thin just to dispel old and erroneous images. I even make sure Meghan always wears Poly Flinders dresses and puts her hair in braids." My sister-in-law turned to me and said, "Being a woman of color, I understand what you are going through. I do the same for my daughter, Jessica, because I want people's sensibilities toward people of color to be different from what they are." This was my "ah-ha moment." We began discussing the multiple layers of this perplexing problem and concluded that the way you think and operate as a mother of a child with Down syndrome, or as a black woman with a black child, is not the way a white person with white children thinks.

Both Kathryn and Rob were sensitive to many issues growing up with Meghan, especially to the language people used and words associated with developmental disabilities. When Kathryn was in high school, her teacher used the word "retarded" as an adjective when describing people who were challenged. Offended, Kathryn raised her hand. "That's not appropriate. My sister has Down syndrome and I don't appreciate that word thrown around." The teacher didn't back down or apologize, and instead said, "It is what it is." Kathryn came home hysterical. I encouraged her to write a letter to the principal and "cc" it to the teacher. No response came from either the principal or the teacher. Offensive language has been my pet peeve, too. I have been at my job for many years, and all the people in my office know about Meghan. One day a coworker was degrading someone she knew and concluded her tirade by saying, "She belongs on a little yellow school bus." I didn't let it go. I don't anymore. "C'mon, Sara," I piped up, "Did you forget?" My intention isn't to embarrass people; I just want them to be aware of their choice of words and learn to discard some of them. To those who have told me I'm too politically correct, I answer, "No! Words can be painful to hear."

Inclusion

When Meghan got to high school, I rallied hard for what was the new buzz in special education – "Full Inclusion." Professionals "in the know" touted that "studies showed inclusion brought more friendships, broader learning, etc." I thought that the stars were aligning for her. This was to be the answer to expanding Meghan's life. I worked hard to get her involved and was oh so hopeful. But all the data wasn't in and these reports were premature. I soon saw her coming home disappointed, upset and frustrated. Then, because you see it's not working, you start thinking that *you're* crazy. "It's the way to go" you were told. I had to step back and take a fresh look. Inclusion really wasn't right, especially for Meghan. I had to learn that it is okay to second guess things even when the "professionals" think they know. Clearly, it is more important that your kid is happy.

Meghan expected to be a part of the *whole* high school experience – all the activities, especially social events – but she was not. She was sure that she would continue as a cheerleader and so looked forward to that, but she was never invited nor included in practices. Never was she asked to any of the school dances much less to her own proms. She lived with dashed hopes and many letdowns. Consequently, my heart was broken all the time. Meghan would come home saying, "Mom, there's a dance tonight." I could only shrug my shoulders and pretend to brush off the searing disappointment knowing that there was nobody with whom she could go. I see now that she is happiest going to any of the dances for people with special needs. It means more because she really *is* a part of that group. Peers are what these kids need, not pretending. Nothing was done viciously; high schoolers did not do anything purposely, it is just the way it was. Full inclusion might be great in theory, but the culture of inclusion had not been promoted or even highlighted in this school and there seemed to be no push to make it work. We were the guinea pigs on that one.

When Meghan graduated from high school in 2003, at the age of 22, the North River Collaborative threw her a monumental party. Even teachers from her early school years came. They not only honored Meghan for being the first one to go through all the Collaborative programs, but also for doing consistently well academically and socially. Having become a well-rounded, well-adjusted, and remarkably independent young adult, Meghan was the town's pride and the Collaborative's role model for success. And here I was standing proudly at a distance, remembering that not so long ago I had envisioned having to hold her hand whenever she crossed the street.

Life After School – Jobs

By the time of Meghan's graduation, my other two children had grown and moved away. It was now Meghan and me. Raising this family alone certainly had its share of trying times, but what helped me get through was reuniting with a guy I had worked with earlier in my life, Steve. We had been friends forever; I wanted to keep it that way so when he talked of marriage I reminded him, "You know, I have a lot of baggage. This is more than most people want to handle." Love won out and we married in 2001. Rob and Kathryn went through a hard time initially, but now they praise him as a stepfather. Meghan loved Steve from the get-go. That affection continues to this day.

Since graduating, Megan has experienced several jobs in the community through her day program. She worked at McDonald's once but came home saying, "I don't want to work there anymore." The reason turned out to be that she was asked to clean the men's room. "I'm uncomfortable," she admitted. I went to the manager and requested she be exempt from that chore, but he explained that it was part of the job. That was it for McDonald's.

Her day program has found her other community jobs. Today, Meghan works at the YMCA two days a week, cleaning the pool area. However, it is not her favorite job; she does not like cleaning. I tell her I do not always like all my jobs either, but "we have to do them." She also has a small office job two days a week, collating and sorting. If you show Meghan a task, she will master it quickly. She is extremely accurate in this work and loves it so much she talks of learning new clerical skills to become an office assistant.

Boyfriends

Meghan's hormones might have spiked in her twenties, but she still yearns for a boyfriend. Fortunately, I am privy to what she is up to because, unbeknownst to Meghan, I can get on her Facebook page. She talks to one employee, Brendan, at the Y all the time, and she texts him often. Despite her persistence, Brendan will kindly reply, "Maybe I'll be able to talk to you tomorrow when I have more time" or "I cannot talk right now." She continues, however, using false snares. "Well, my friend's father just died." Brendan isn't lured in and tries to back off politely. "I'm sorry for that," he will say, "but I'll talk another time."

130

As her mom, I will not interfere, but I do try to keep on top of her social activity. She was a girlfriend at one point to Sam, a fellow client at her day program. He acts out a lot there and has been restrained many times. She was also a girlfriend to a young man named Robby, but then she broke *his* heart. That is Meghan's life – lots of drama. It is like living in a soap opera. In Special Olympics there is a young man she is a girlfriend to now. His name is David; they call him "Hollywood" – a sure indication of what attracts her.

Meghan's desire to have a boyfriend is waning as she ages. That is not to say she is done wanting a relationship.

Social Life

Lori came into Meghan's life through her day program. She loved Meghan and took her under her wing. Lori would take Meghan to the mall, to her bowling league and weekly dances on the South Shore. Lori also invited Meghan to participate in a choir practice she started for people with special needs and even made special dates for sleepovers. Meghan remembers all of these outings fondly but her greatest memories are of the yearly cruises Lori and her husband Vinny took her on. They meant the world to her

Meghan and Lori's daughter Amy, who has physical disabilities, spent lots of time together. They would go to the mall and Meghan would push Amy around for hours in her wheelchair. Meghan has the best memories of spending time with Lori and Amy; all three members of Lori's family were a very important part of Meghan's life.

Just a few years ago, Steve and I decided to take Meghan to Disneyworld for her vacation. Despite our efforts to make this trip special for Meghan – including finding a fabulous hotel with a pool and making sure she was the only focus of our attention for a week – both Steve and I realized it was not fun for her to go with us. Meghan would have been happier with her peers.

131

Growing Up and Moving Out

From the beginning, in every IEP (Individual Education Plan) and every ISP (Individual Service Plan), I made sure goals were established for Meghan's further independence. I have always wanted the optimum life for her and knew that this would eventually mean that Meghan would live on her own. After Meghan's graduation in 2003, I wrote letter after letter to DDS (Department of Developmental Disabilities) pressuring them to find her suitable housing, learning from other parents that getting anyone into a group home is a lengthy ordeal. Recently, there had been a settlement in a long standing legal case involving housing for adults with developmental disabilities. Friends of mine with older sons and daughters were finally able to move them into new group homes that began sprouting up on the South Shore as a result of the lawsuit. That legal battle took ten years to resolve for these families; in the back of my mind, I figured I had ten years.

Housing for Meghan became more and more of a concern because she was often at home for long stretches between jobs. Every day at work, all day, I worried. I was not concerned about house fires or other emergencies, but I was terrified of people, especially strangers, coming to the door. Meghan knew to lock the doors; she knew to call 911 and was constantly drilled about not opening the door for anyone. I told her not to even look out the window if the doorbell buzzed: "Just call me!" To this day, I do not know whether or not she would open the door if someone knocked. She is smart about many things, but when it comes to people and their agendas, she does not always read them correctly.

My angst hit an all-time high when I learned that there was a sex offender in our neighborhood. I went to the police station to find out if there were any others nearby, knowing they are everywhere. Apparently, another one had moved in down the street from us. That made two of them, two level-three sex offenders within a mile of our house. I decided that is enough and wrote a letter to DDS telling them that because I had to go to work to keep a roof over our head, Meghan could not be in this house alone given the danger in our neighborhood. DDS heeded my alarm.

In July 2008, I received the call from DDS saying, "we have two young ladies who are going to live together in an apartment with three bedrooms; we think Meghan is a perfect match here." Startled, I found myself hesitating, but agreed to look at it. When I arrived, I met Mary, the mother of one of the other two girls. She worked next door to this apartment house and could walk across the street to see her daughter. Mary had gotten used to her daughter Ginny living elsewhere, as she had moved out some time ago. However, after nearly 30 years of having Meghan home, the thought of her leaving was unnerving and frightening. However, I felt pressured to take this opportunity, sensing that a similar opportunity might not happen again, at least not shortly. I was not ready but decided I could always bring Meghan home if her new living situation did not work. Despite feeling overwhelmed and unprepared, I went forward.

My first step was to throw a shower for Meghan on my back deck. This party was planned so quickly that I inadvertently forgot to invite some wonderful friends. People responded to the invitation immediately, some saying they would not miss it for the world. Over 50 people showed up to surprise her. Meghan was so overcome seeing everyone that she burst into tears. I had never seen such emotion from her.

The theme for her shower was Hannah Montana. Sheets, towels, pillowcases and anything else you might need when you move into your place was emblazoned with images of Ms. Montana. Meghan moved out two months later, in August 2008. I did not have much time to get ready for this emotionally.

I left her at her new home and pretended to be strong. "If you need me, I will get in this car and see you in a minute. You are just down the street." She might have been homesick for a short period, but I was a wreck! Meghan quickly fell into the routine at her new place. She never called to say, "Come get me," and the instances on the phone of her saying, "I miss you," became fewer very quickly. Within a year she was completely comfortable.

The first night without her was awful. Even now, I can well up just thinking about it. I want her home; I want her back living with me, but I know that it is not the best thing for her. She is happier with company, and I am away a lot since I work long hours. Sometimes, I will call and ask, "Do you want to come home for the weekend and go to the movies?" She will say, "Nope, I'm just gonna hang here." This did not happen right off the bat, but it was soon obvious that she was creating her own little life and I had to realize it no longer involved me. That was tough. It came too quickly. Much to my delight, Meghan still phones me twice a night. The last call is just to say, "I love you! Good night."

Reality of Life in a Group Home

In Meghan's apartment there is a kitchen, a living room, and a bedroom for each of the girls: Pat, Ginny and Meghan. One of her housemates, Ginny, has physical disabilities and is assigned a PCA at all times, so someone is in the apartment with them 24/7.

It is still a challenge to make sure that Meghan is getting all of the services she is entitled to receive. We are supposed to sit down each year for her ISP (Individual Service Plan) meeting, which I understand should be a discussion about Meghan and her needs for the upcoming year. Instead, the plans are usually drafted without any input from me and presented for my signature, which I find extremely frustrating.

More importantly, I am concerned about the staffing hours assigned to Meghan by DDS. It is minimal – ten hours a week. This might have worked when she lived at home and I took her everywhere, but in a group home her social life depends on those ten hours, which get eaten into quickly for grocery shopping, picking up prescriptions and other errands. I have pleaded with Meghan's case worker for more time. Every time I see Meghan sitting around doing nothing, I pick up the phone to plead my case for more hours. Meghan has Mass Health PCA hours, but they are to be used strictly for medical reasons and cannot be used for social outings. I sought out these PCA hours years ago; they were a stroke of luck. Without them, well, I imagine she would have to come home.

Other ongoing issues that I bring up at the yearly ISP meeting, and which have yet to be solved, include concerns about the effectiveness of the employees in the house, issues involving the three girls, and Meghan's weight gain.

The staff in the apartment is in charge of making meals. In her short time there, Meghan, whose weight I have always struggled to maintain, has put on 40 pounds. At one point, when she lived at home, Meghan got a bit heavy so I put her on Weight Watchers, which worked because it offers a well-balanced diet. Another huge factor with Weight Watchers is that Meghan did not feel like she was deprived of foods because you can eat most anything, in moderation. The staff has put her back on the Weight Watchers diet, but she is still gaining weight. I know I cannot solely blame the staff because Meghan will always find ways to sneak sodas and candy bars. However, I cannot help but notice that all three girls in the house have put on the pounds. The staff does not seem to realize how important it is to cook nutritious meals, ones less laden with gravies and sauces. The staff loves it when Meghan is happy and Meghan is most happy when she is eating.

I asked Meghan what she had for lunch this past week. She was able to recall that on three days she went to work with peanut butter and jelly sandwiches, and one day she had a hot dog. When I bring up my concern about her diet, the supervisor tells me that Meghan has "Rights." "With *her* money, it's *her* choice to buy and eat what *she* wants."

When she lived at home, Meghan was active and loved to go to dances on Friday night. Steve and I would bring her to them, go out to dinner ourselves nearby, and pick her up afterwards. I would also bring her to the health club, where she would spend time primping and out-fitting herself in all the right gym clothes with matching headbands just to get on the treadmill. She was sure all the boys were looking at her. I would take her a few days a week to an outdoor track, give her head-phones tuned to fast music and, while I ran, she would move about.

I continue to encourage the staff to get Meghan moving. Every time I go to the house I question the i-Pad I bought for Meghan and wonder how I can take it away. Using the i-Pad is such a sedentary activity. She is becoming addicted to it, and to her phone. If somebody would sit with her and teach her different things on the internet, that would be different. She is very interested in social media and how to do things on the computer. We just went to the Apple Store so she could find out how to transfer pictures to her i-Pad. She is on Facebook and enjoys reading emails and texts. This could be an opportunity to teach her more about spelling, but I know that is not happening. Instead, she goes into her room with the i-Pad and stays on it all night watching movies. I also worry about what's coming in on her computer that might entice her.

Ideally, Meghan should be out of the house a couple of nights a week and some part of Sundays. (My sister, Jean, picks her up on Sat-urday mornings and I see her later on Saturdays, often taking her out for dinner.) I would love to know she is going bowling, meeting other people who live in different group homes – anything but lazing around. Classes through the local ARC (Association for Retarded Citizens) would also be something valuable for the house to look into offering. Meghan loves to sing and her confidence in this area is remarkable. She would love singing classes; they might even help! She truly thinks she is Britney Spears. I would also love to see her back at weekly and monthly dances; she loves them, and can she move! Meghan watches endless dance videos and copies them. Her rhythm is incredible. Whenever we go to weddings, everyone wants to dance with Meghan. She is fun to watch.

Meghan does have the YMCA written on her schedule for exercise each week, but she is happiest when she gets to stay home and put on her comfy clothes. Like everyone, Meghan needs this downtime, but I do not want to see her isolate, which she tends to do. Once Meghan is at an activity, she loves it.

Other Empty Promises

Although Meghan likes living in her group home, there are some ongoing frustrations. Wondering if another house may be a better fit, I asked recently, "Meghan, if the opportunity came up to move to another house, would you like that?" "No, I think I would rather stay where I am, get a little more independent and then live by myself." Sounds great, but NO! First of all, she does not get enough hours for the necessary support she would need to live by herself. Furthermore, living alone would be unhealthy for her; she needs stimulation and transportation to any event she would like to attend.

Ideally, I would like Marj, the supervisor of Meghan's group home, to send a directive to the house staff to plan outings and incorporate more activities for the girls, even if it is just a walk in the afternoon. Then, I want to see the staff carry through and make this a standard routine.

Future Concerns

I am thinking ahead to when I get older. I am not crazy about Meghan living at such a distance. Rob and Kathryn live elsewhere and are creating lives for themselves, as they should be. Not only is Meghan far from me, but she is far from her work as well. She spends an inordinate amount of time in a van commuting more than 60 minutes each way because they pick others up en route.

This leads me to my last concern for Meghan – her vocational life. Are the skills she needs to acquire to meet her hopes of becoming an office assistant being addressed? She works at her day program's office job four hours a week. Her other job, cleaning at the YMCA, is also four hours a week. Eight hours a week is not much vocational time, and only four of the hours are in the area she wants to pursue. The rest of her 20 hours is spent in the day program's in-house component, but this is not preparing her for the job she wants. What's more, she does not like being in-house. There is much drama there, and she sees too much. Meghan gets visibly upset witnessing the number of client outbursts, to say nothing of the number of subsequent restraints. Her discomfort is obvious and real. She has spoken up, but the answer she has been given is, "You don't need to stay here while this is going on. You can go use my office or sit in a quiet room where there is no drama." I am not sure this is the best use of her time.

There is also a high staff turnover at her day program, so consistency is an issue. It is hard when someone gets to know Meghan, begins to find how to work with her, and then leaves. One supervisor had Meghan pegged. When she announced she was leaving, I asked her first to make sure the next case manager learned of Meghan's propensity for drama and, second, to pass on her strategies to handle Meghan. I do not know if that was done.

My concerns are real and there are many. All affect who she is becoming and shape the next phase of Meghan's life. I wonder what other parents do, or what they can let go of. I wonder what would happen if I was not here to advocate for Meghan.

Despite some of these disheartening and persistent realities, moving out and being on her own has made a significant impact on Meghan's sense of self-worth. It was not noticeable right away, but I see a different Meghan today. When she lived at home she would do whatever I was doing, but now she makes decisions for her own life. I have seen such maturation over the last seven years that sometimes I have to ask, "Who is this person?"

As for an overall comment on group homes, I look at myself as a trailblazer for DDS. I am always questioning things and constantly asking how come *this* is not there? Is it just me who sees what is missing? Am I the only one concerned about weight gain and inactivity? Is it just me who wants community and social programming to be a focus? I sense all parents want that sense of belonging for their child.

There are plenty of older people now with Down syndrome, yet there are no programs for them. Most of the activities out there are for younger people. We need a new tier of support for this older group. I see my friend in her late seventies down at the mall with her son who has Down syndrome. He should have some place to go with his peers, instead of having to hang out at the mall with his mother. However, that is what I was doing that same day – taking Meghan down to the mall to let her wander around in her favorite store, FYE, while I sat outside.

As a parent, I am as alone today as I was in the beginning of Meghan's life and once again, I am lost for answers. I want someone to pave the way for me, but it is not in the cards. Am I expected to design the programs for this age group? I do not know if I would be able to, but I could let people know what is important and what works. Simply put, Meghan needs to continue to participate in her life, and not isolate herself. Like all of us, she needs to feel useful and she needs people. Wouldn't it be great if she also had something to look forward to? As for me, I will continue to advocate for Meghan and hope her siblings will take over when I no long can.

Chapter Five

Jane Carey and Derrick

I never wanted children. I was an only child and heard enough of my parents' lives to know that having children complicated things. Plus, my career was going well and my marriage of nearly ten years to Joe was happily rolling along. But that life took a quick turn in 1979 and strangely, it resulted in a shift in thinking. My sister-in-law Eileen, at the age of 27, had just been killed in a car accident. Her husband, Billy, needed to take a second job to pay off, of all things, the car she was killed in. I stepped in to become the replacement mother for their five-year-old daughter, Jennifer, from Friday night until Sunday. This arrangement went on for two years until Billy got back on his feet but, funny, by then I did not want to lose Jennifer. She had taught me that I *could* be a mother.

Joe had desperately wanted children, but years of suffering through my endometriosis only reinforced the thinking that a child was not in the cards for us. However, life has a funny way of moving you around. Just after those two years ended with Jennifer, I miraculously conceived. I was 29, just shy of 30, and now I was thrilled. But something bizarre began. For some reason I started praying and found myself, throughout the next nine months, repeating the same prayer in earnest over and over and over again and out loud. "Please God, not an ugly baby; Please God, not Down syndrome." I am not overly religious so where that came from and why I said it *every* day to everyone I worked with I cannot tell you.

Three weeks before his due date, I went into labor for a hellish 30-plus hours at the Brigham and Women's Hospital, where I worked. It was March 3, and I said to Joe, "Hmmm 3/3 – that might be a good date." Then the clock went around and it was March 4. I thought, okay 3…4, that has a nice ring. Finally, in the middle of the night, I delivered and remember an RN saying, "You have a beautiful little platinum blond boy here." I asked, "Ten fingers and ten toes?" "Yup, ten fingers and ten toes," she answered.

I was taken back to the labor room and Joe followed. Once there, I asked him where the baby was and he said that the doctor just wanted to check something out about his eyes. "Oh," I said. Shortly, an RN and MD walked into my room, shoulder to shoulder. The wheels in my head started to turn. The RN handed me the baby as the doctor started to speak, but each word was labored and agonizingly slow. I wondered if he had taken Valium. He began, "We are reeeealllly not sure, we are going to do further testing." I began to realize something was wrong. I glanced down and for the first time in his little life this baby opened his eyes and looked at me. It was in a flash, that moment, the sight of his eyes that told me the whole story. I screamed out, "OH MY GOD, DOWN SYNDROME." "Please," I shouted, "just tell me that all babies look this way and that it will go away. Please, tell me something." But I already knew. I could hear a needle drop in the room. Joe stood staring at me and the doctor and nurse were completely silenced.

My body went numb. Derrick was less than an hour old and all I could think was that I would never be able to smile again. Along with that thought, was a vision in my mind of a huge marquis with upper case lettering. I was sure its bright lights would always be blinking, "DOWN SYNDROME."

My OBGYN had heard me talk about my unusual daily prayer but had confidently said, "Jane, you're not in that age range, there's no history of this in your family. You're being ridiculous; there's no risk." He could hardly look at me when Derrick was born.

Joe, too, was in disbelief. "I don't even know if I love him," he said gruffly. "Okay," I said, "whatever you want, we'll do." Silently, I was hoping he would urge me to give him up. But my next thought was, "I'm going to be a single mother." I realized then and there that if my husband had any misgivings or any kind of negative attitude, I would do this alone. There is no way I was going to give this child up; I grew this baby. The bonding was that instantaneous. I even remember thinking that if anybody tried to attack me leaving the hospital with Derrick – the area around the Brigham was not so safe at that time –

the mugger would end up in the hospital, not me. This sense of protection was so strong and extended to eliminating anything in my way, including my husband if need be.

Soon, the chief neurologist of Brigham and Women's came in to my room and spoke to me, staring at his shoes the whole time. "I don't know why," he began, "but mothers of these children tell me that they get more out of them than their normal children. I don't understand it but all I can do is to tell you that I hear this time and time again." I thanked him.

Nothing comforted me. Knowing I was committed did not erase the emotional torment. I remember another pediatrician coming in saying, "It used to be not too long ago that babies like this would be put away." I sat up, hoping my life was going to return to normal, sure that he was about to say, "So there's a place up in Danvers..." Please! I thought. He went on very matter-of-factly saying, "They don't do that anymore," never adding anything positive like, "because they can learn so much."

I called my mother from the hospital. "Oh, this is so exciting!" she said. "NO, stop, stop, stop," I interrupted, "there is something wrong." "What do you mean?" she asked. "He has Down syndrome." "I don't know what that means," she screamed. "The word you would know, Mom, would be Mongoloid." She shrieked into the phone and hung up.

My father, hearing the news, was also distraught. He kept storming into my hospital room shrieking, "I survived two years of POW camp. Now, you have my curse." For the first time in my life I saw my big, strong, Italian father burst into tears. He had been given up at birth by his mother and never felt like he belonged; much of his life had been odd and tumultuous. His mother would come in and out anytime she needed a loan. It was all very sad.

Not only did my father keep insisting that I had his curse, and not only did I have to witness his incredible sorrow, but he also started experiencing chest pains. I began to think that I am going to kill my father and be blamed for his heart attack all because of the baby I just had.

Derrick ended up under UV light for several days because he was jaundiced. At night I would go in and watch him sleep and I would cry for every child that had not been held or loved because they were Down syndrome.

The Phone

My friend, Dusty, knew what to say to me. At the time she was a social worker counseling pregnant teenagers at St. Margaret's, the maternity hospital in Dorchester. The morning after the birth, she called me from work and I told her the news. Dusty turned immediately to the co-worker next to her and said, "I have to leave. My best friend just had a baby with Down syndrome." Dusty spent the next few days curled up in the corner chair in my hospital room. Her presence was a gift by itself, but she went a step further and made the first call to Eunice, a fellow social worker running the Down syndrome program at Children's Hospital. That was a call I never wanted to be making. Dusty also had a few links to other mothers of babies with special needs and left me with their phone numbers. I did not know what I was looking for; I just wanted to talk to anyone who had a child with a disability.

Word traveled to Children's Hospital next door, where I had trained years before. My old boss, Nancy, came over and said to me, "Janie, don't you remember? You had a thing for these kids with Down syndrome. Remember? When they were coming in through the clinic you asked specifically to follow them every month." At the time, 1971, I was involved in a Children's Hospital clinic started by a pediatrician, Dr. Siegfried M. Pueschel M.D., PH.D, J.D., M.P.H.* We would see a fair amount of children with Down syndrome ranging in age from one to five years old. I was drawn to them then but could not say that it comforted me now. Nancy, too, left me with a few phone numbers of mothers who had children with Down syndrome.

A geneticist came to my room from Mass General. He had xeroxed a copy of a book that he held up and told me I should buy. The title of this black book was *Mongolism,* written in large, lime green letters. It was a huge, textbook-sized book – and the title was screaming at me. Speaking of a marquis! I turned the book over to find a picture

---

*Dr. Pueschel was a pioneer in the world of Down syndrome after having a son, Christian, born with it. He went on to become the director of the first comprehensive Down syndrome program in the country at Boston's Children's Hospital. At the time, Dr. Pueschel was also running a double-blind study to dispute (and eventually disprove) the theory of another doctor in Florida who was claiming that high doses of vitamin therapy would cure Down syndrome. Over his lifetime, Dr. Pueschel wrote numerous books on children with Down syndrome.

of a 300-pound girl with Down syndrome, on a swing, wearing a Girl Scout uniform. Crying and laughing at the same time. I asked, "Is this supposed to make me feel better?"

Because I could not sleep, because I was crying, I read. I read and I cried. When the geneticist left I scanned the pages he gave me and was horrified to see pictures of kids in hospital johnnies on institutional floors. I also remember the book saying that you will fight every hour of every day to try to teach them to do things for themselves up to the age of seven, and then no matter how hard you work, they are going to start regressing. How could I ever smile after reading that? I detested that book.

As I lay in the hospital, all I could think to do was call the phone number Dusty left me for the clinic at Children's. Every time I dialed the number for help, however, I began sobbing and would have to hang up and try again. Finally, the clinic's social worker, Eunice, came over and helped me fill out the necessary paperwork to register Derrick. Even seeing a kind face like hers made me weep. I told her about the frightening book the geneticist had suggested I purchase. The next day, when she was with me again, the geneticist coincidently came back. I introduced him to Eunice and together we told him not to show his book to any other mother who had a new baby with Down syndrome. The doctor was caught off guard and began emphasizing its scientific merits. "Yes, perhaps," Eunice said "the genetics might be fine, but there are better books or pamphlets that will offer the same genetic information, and are updated for new mothers."

A day after Derrick was born, Joe came back into my room. "I cried for a day," he said, "and then I thought about my sister who died so young and the mother I just lost. This is my baby; I am going to take care of him." He was over the shock of Derrick in 24 hours. I remained, on the other hand, hysterical for a long time. This would annoy him, but he did not have the hormonal thing going on, nor did he have the marquis lit up in his head.

Still in the hospital, a man appeared at the door with his son. His wife just had a baby and she heard I was beside myself. She encouraged her husband to bring in their four-year-old with Down syndrome. He also brought me pamphlets and phone numbers for the various ARCs (Association for Retarded Citizens). I could only read them and weep.

My days in the hospital seemed endless. I could not get out of my own way and it seemed nobody had a positive thing to say. A nursing assistant knew I was trying to heal and one day brought me a poem called, *Heaven's Very Special Child** by Edna Massimilla.

Heaven's Very Special Child

A meeting was held quite far from Earth
It was time again for another birth.
Said the Angels to the Lord above –
"This special child will need much love.
Her progress may be very slow
Accomplishment she may not show.
And she'll require extra care
From the folks she meets down there.
She may not run or laugh or play
Her thoughts may seem quite far away
So many times she will be labeled
different, helpless and disabled.
So, let's be careful where she's sent.
We want her life to be content.
Please, Lord, find the parents who
Will do a special job for you.
They will not realize right away
The leading role they are asked to play.
But with this child sent from above
Comes stronger faith, and richer love.
And soon they'll know the privilege given
In caring for their gift from heaven.
Their precious charge, so meek and mild
Is heaven's very special child."

* *Heaven's Very Special Child* was written and copyrighted in 1956 by Edna Massimilla of Hatboro, PA, about her daughter, Ruth, born with Down syndrome in 1952. It was printed in Ann Landers' syndicated newspaper column. In 2006, Abigail Van Buren (Dear Abbey) spoke with Edna, then age 90. She explained that she wrote the poem to emphasize that every creation is for a purpose. The poem was read and acknowledged by President Kennedy on the day of his assassination.

I cried of course, reading this, but something clicked. It was as though I finally found someone who might understand what I am feeling. I wrote to her and gave her high accolades for what she was able to put on paper. She responded very formally. The Massimillas were told that their third daughter, Ruth, was a mongoloid and they were encouraged to "throw her out"; instead they took her home. Edna's husband, John, went back to the seminary after Ruth was born. The two served as the chaplains at Delaware's Institution for Retarded Children. The following was John's poem.

She thinks no evil, does no harm.
Her disposition is always calm,
So full of love and kindness, too,
She only sees the good in you.
Anger, lust, they're not real.
Such normal impulses she doesn't feel
She is innocent. This is true –
Of hate and fear and things we do.
Such perfect trust, so hard to find,
Exemplifies her peace of mind.
With eyes upturned and heart sincere,
Her thoughts may seem quite far from here.
A deeper knowledge, yet not expressed,
Perhaps she's wiser than the rest.
She's sweet and gentle, meek and mild,
She's our lovely Down syndrome child.

I clung to these as my new life raft.

Home

The hospital kept me for five days because I was not healing, but finally, when Derrick's jaundice improved, we went home. All I could do there was more of the same: read the literature I had accumulated and cry. From Nancy, Dusty and the man who brought in his son and the pamphlets on the ARC, I now had a full folder of information and quite a few phone numbers. Back then people answered their phones, there was no caller ID and companies did not *robo* call you. There was also no voicemail; people simply picked up the receiver. Frequently, however, I dialed a number and burst into tears the second someone answered. I am going to guess that those who put their name on lists and heard someone sobbing on the other end of the phone knew that the call had something to do with Down syndrome. I remember calling one woman just because I liked the sound of her name.

One call would often lead to another list of phone numbers. Out of concern, it seemed, people would tell people who would tell people. One of my teary calls led to an unexpected visit. A man brought his whole family by our house just so I could see that they were managing fine with their youngest child (Down syndrome) in tow. "I am getting divorced," this father announced, "but I'm going to make sure I see this guy all the time," he said while tussling his son's hair. "We just had him skiing," he said proudly. I sighed and thought, "Okay, they do fit in."

Yet, I was so, so fragile. As quickly as a glimmer of hope like this would shine, I could be completely undone by the next thought, "DOWN SYNDROME," alighting in my head. And sure enough, that is exactly what happened. The young boy suddenly tugged on his father's shirt and whispered, "I have to go pee-pee." Immediately I sank; this boy, five or six years old, still needed toileting help. I panicked. Endless toilet training, I now saw, would be just one more stumbling block. Raising him was surely going to be impossible.

I was living in a nightmare. I wasn't suicidal but I would wake up and think "Oh damn, I am still alive."

When I could not stop crying, I was first given Valium. My neurologist, seeing me still in tears months later, commented, "You're really having a hard time with this." Frankly, I was surprised that he was surprised. Nobody seemed to understand that this was the deepest, darkest, dankest time.

I was prone to migraines and had been put on a therapeutic dose of Elavil to ward them off. My doctor suggested increasing the medication to an anti-depressant level. "Let's see if this helps you." Soon, I was not crying every second; I could periodically think about Down syndrome without becoming hysterical. I had not felt any of the side effects from increasing the medicine, but a few days in, when Derrick fell asleep in my arms, I got up to lay him down. In my usual hurried manner, I took five giant steps and went crashing down onto the floor, hitting my head along the way. I could feel myself going down, all the while trying to catch Derrick. (Joe told me later that it looked like I threw the baby into the air.) When I came to, there was Joe and the baby crying. Joe was pacing feverishly, repeating, "My poor baby, my poor baby." He thought I tripped and accused me of being clumsy. I lay there for a minute trying to figure out what had just happened. Fortunately, with a bit of medical knowledge, I realized that blood simply did not get to my brain. "Joe, what are you yelling at me for? I fainted." That put an end to that elevated dosage of Elavil, but I faced a torturous juggling act to get the right balance for my depression and the migraines.

Friends and Neighbors and Parents

Coming home, my phone was fairly quiet; friends did not know what to say to me and instead asked others. Who was not quiet was my neighbor. Rhonda was just trying to be friendly, but she talked too much and what was coming out of her mouth should not have been. She would grab a couple of kids in the neighborhood and tell them, "Did you hear Mrs. Carey had a baby? The baby is Down syndrome; go tell your mother, tell your father." I finally asked her to simply let people know that I had the baby.

She also had quirky ideas. She insisted that Derrick was born with Down syndrome because I had gotten confirmed in the Catholic Church just before having him. Despite trying to explain that Down syndrome happens at the moment of conception – not confirmation – she was relentless in telling me this.

My parents were as supportive as they could be when we first got home. They were sure, however, that Derrick would be gorked forever and they were under the belief that children like this should go away because "they were never going to learn." My father's acceptance, while not as quick as my husband's 24-hour turnaround, did come. His came abruptly and unexpectedly.

My dad was an agent to a jockey at Suffolk Downs. For years he was at the race track six hours a day after his regular job running his grocerette in Dorchester. Shortly after Derrick was born, he ran into a priest at the track, one of the many people he knew there. After saying their hellos, my father burst into tears and, for some reason, began telling the priest about his unrelenting cursed life. "I was a prisoner of war, my mother abandoned me at birth, my childhood was terrible and now, my daughter just gave birth to a baby with Down syndrome." His tears gushed as he finally spit out, "She's got my curse." The priest, having quietly stood there listening, simply asked, "What about the baby, Ed? Are you thinking about the baby?"

My father suddenly became intrigued by Derrick, driving a great distance almost daily just to stare at him in his infant seat on the kitchen table. If Derrick was startled by a noise, my father would delight. "Look at that, he's reacting." My father never wanted to do any of the food prep or change his diaper, but as soon as the bottle was ready he grabbed it to feed him, hoping to see that Derrick's suck had improved.

My mother came a little less often and in a separate car because she was never on time and my father felt he had an important schedule to keep. When my mom arrived, I would have to stop everything and cater to her; she was absolutely no help.

My father, understanding the demands of a new baby, would leave our house at a reasonable hour, knowing we had to work the next day. But my mother was oblivious, and she would stay forever. It got to the point where they would call in the morning to say they were coming and I wanted to say, "Oh no, please don't come again, not today. I am tired, I have to heal." (I was still depressed and had those phone calls to make.)

But down they would come; my father often being the one to bring dinner for Joe and me. He thought of and did the things that my mother should have been thinking about but did not, ever. He would ask questions about Derrick that never dawned on her, and he would look for things about Derrick that she could have cared less about.

I have always been aware of my mother's deficits and shortcomings. At 5 pm every night, all through my childhood and adolescence, she would suddenly have a headache and reach for the Anacin. It would take her hours to pull dinner together – while I starved. We would end up eating dinner at 8 pm, when I should have been getting ready for bed.

In time, my mother did become more interested in Derrick and was especially good at buying books, reading them to him and discussing the pictures. She nurtured, but not to the extent of my father. Derrick, however, felt love from both and over time Derrick became their favored grandchild.

Moving Forward

Derrick was evaluated for the Down syndrome program at Children's when he was a month old. The clinic day was divided into 40-minute segments and included pediatric evaluations as well as speech, physical and occupational therapy. You would meet other parents during the four or five hours you spent there each month, but the schedule was so tight you could only say a few sentences to each other as you passed between sessions.

The clinic did not do enough of what I hoped it would do. It was nice to see other people participating, but there was never any chance for group discussion or time to listen to others and put our heads together. I was still in such a state of grief and needed to see someone else feeling what I was feeling or hear someone tell me that they once felt like I did. That never happened.

Right out of the hospital I was not only involved in the clinic at Children's but was also part of an Early Infant Stimulation Program, a government program that has since been defunded. An RN from the program would come to the house once a week, and an OT would visit twice a week to show me how to play with Derrick in a more stimulating and productive way. How would I have known that if I rang a rattle on his right side he would turn to look for it and, in so doing, strengthen his weak neck muscles? As it was, I spent three months coddling his poor little, wobbly neck.

I was hyper-aware of Derrick's every move and eagerly looked for progress, so I referred to Dr. Spock. Every time I noted Spock's timeframe for developmental milestones, my heart would break. No child with Down syndrome was anywhere near those markers. I had no gauge for Derrick until Dr. Pueschel finally came out with one, giving much wider age variances. This helped decrease my worn-out mantra, "Oh no, you can't even do this yet!"

Derrick continued to be followed. When I went back to my four-day work schedule, I would drive him into the clinic at Children's on my day off. He needed everything I could give him, I thought. Perhaps, if I did all that was humanly possible...perhaps...it would increase his intelligence. That was always the question and it was always my motive. I could not let up; I did not even want him to nap. When I would shower I would take him into the bathroom with me and reach around the curtain to shake the infant seat or call to him if I saw he nodded off.

Infants, of course, need to sleep and Derrick did not sleep more than any other baby, but I was afraid; I did not want him to lose a minute.

Derrick slept in a cradle in our room. I would be woken up by all sorts of grunting and snorting noises; I could not figure out what they were about. (Truthfully, I did not think Derrick was even capable of doing much or feeling things without me.) I would climb out of bed and find that he had worked himself up into the corner of the cradle; I thought he did it by mistake. After I fed him, I would place him back in carefully, smack in the middle of the cradle where I thought it most comfortable, but the noises would start once more. I would get up again and find him back in the cradle's corner. It finally dawned on me that he felt secure with his head against something. Of course, he had just been leaning against *me* for the last nine months! He was simply being a baby.

I was a new mother, sure, but there was so much about Derrick that was unknown. Between his rumbling noises and his difficulty breathing, I thought I would never sleep again. His nasal passages, like others with Down syndrome, were much narrower than normal, making him sound "snorkley," like he constantly had to blow his nose. I gave him Triaminic on the advice of my old-fashioned pediatrician. However, Derrick was prone to frequent colds, and they seemed to be worsening.

I mentioned this at the clinic and they recommended Derrick see an ENT. In late November we met Dr. Magoon, who ordered a chest X-ray because Derrick was "juicy," a word used when referring to patients who needed to be suctioned. In our follow-up with him, Dr. Magoon, in his haughty way, reported that he had found nothing of concern. Derrick, however, continued to be very sick and six weeks later he was back again as an emergency admission at Children's.

Despite feeling that I needed to be with Derrick every minute, I had no choice but to go back to work at Brigham and Women's Hospital in Boston after four months. We found a young woman, Mary, to take care of him. It was Mary who, through a simple tickle on his cheek, provoked Derrick's first smile. On another memorable day, this one in December, Mary called, saying "Derrick seems to be having trouble breathing." I started firing questions, which finally led to, "Is he blue at all?" She said, "Just around his lips." That was it. I ran to get my car, drove through the gnarly Boston streets, beat my way through the South Shore traffic only to grab him and get him back to Children's. I drove right by the exit for the local hospital, knowing that we would have been stuck in the waiting room. The whole way up to Boston I kept shaking his little arm, saying, "Keep breathing, sweetheart, keep breathing." (This was before any laws prohibiting baby seats in the front seat.) The staff in the emergency room was quick, especially when I told them he was having difficulty breathing.

It was Christmastime – the first Christmas of Derrick's life – and he had atelectasis, a partially collapsed lung. The doctors, being very thorough, looked over his records and noted that he had a chest X-ray just six weeks earlier. They reviewed it and were aghast to see that pneumonia, or bronchiolitis as they called it then, had gone untreated. They told me that the ENT owed me an explanation. I cornered Dr. Magoon in the hallway one day and when I questioned this grave oversight, he answered, "Well, I was looking from here up," pointing to his throat area. "I am an ENT after all." "But," I argued, "*you* ordered a chest X-ray." He responded angrily, as if I was going to sue him. "What do you want from me?" "I just want you to take care of my child," I answered. If I was facing this then, with what little knowledge I had, I cannot imagine what parents before me faced. But, this is where I had been brought to – using an angry, assertive, "in-your-face" style. I was to repeat this approach again, whenever I felt I had to.

Derrick was put into an oxygen tent and stayed there for two weeks. I had to crawl into it just to hold him, even talk to him. All of this, and he was only nine months old. I remember quietly going in to see him, his bed slanted upwards to keep him breathing. Tears poured out of my eyes. One of the pediatricians came over and dabbed at my face. "Your baby is going to be fine," he said assuredly.

Joe and I were just getting used to Derrick and here we were, thinking he was going to be taken from us.

Finding Helen

Mary was okay but looking back over that incident I was not thrilled; she should have called me hours earlier, before he was blue. Mary remained with us a little longer while I wracked my brain for someone to replace her. I left a note for our wonderful housekeeper, Eva, asking if she knew anyone who might be interested in taking Mary's job. Eva's mother, Helen, it turned out, needed extra "pin" money and was interested in working for us. We let Mary go, and happily put Derrick into Helen's hands. Helen stayed with us until her death on February 11, 2014, when Derrick was just shy of his thirty-second birthday. Initially, we called her Helen but soon called her Auntie Helen. Later, we simplified it to Auntie and eventually, adoringly, we called her Ma. Her whole family was involved with Derrick from the beginning. This was Helen's way. She had a sister who had a drinking problem, and Helen ended up raising this sister's three children. They were grown by the time Derrick came along, and Helen was excited by the notion of having a baby again.

It was later that Helen admitted her initial apprehension. "I thought I was going to have to treat Derrick like a China doll, but he is just like any other little boy." From the get-go, Helen was my strength. I was in her room when she passed, that is how close she was to all of us. Since her passing, Eva continues to periodically pick Derrick up and take him for the day.

Finding My Way Up and Out

Even with the gift of Helen in our lives, I was still so very sad; aching for something, I knew not what. There were no personal computers at the time; mail was *the* mode of communication. I kept writing small checks, subscribing to anything and everything that came with the words Down syndrome on it. I was soon inundated with information – and more phone numbers. In one subscription called *Sharing our Caring*, I read dozens of stories written by parents of children with Down syndrome; some were really good. My heart broke for a woman whose husband walked out on the day of their child's diagnosis. As bad as I thought I had it, I saw that it could always be worse.

While that life lesson was made clear, I was also slowly realizing that I could not dwell on my own misery. Shuffling through the mountains of paperwork I had accumulated, I happened on a booklet, published by the National Down Syndrome Society, called *This Baby Needs You Even More*. Its cover featured an irresistible face of an adoring father holding his son with Down syndrome. With his eyes closed and his nose squished against the baby's cheek, he snuggled his bright-eyed baby to his chest. I opened to read the first sentence, "Congratulations on the birth of your baby." Why that hit me, I don't know, but dawn broke. It is so simple, I realized. My Derrick is *just* a baby. Inside were one-sentence testimonials straight from the mouths of parents:

"Of course there's pain and hard work with a Down syndrome child. But what makes you think that there isn't pain and hard work with any children?"

"There's no reason to believe your Down syndrome child won't read, but you have to forget the timetable. Put it right out of your head. They'll do everything, but it will just take longer."

"You never know what your child is capable of. There's such a range with Down syndrome kids."

The statements were so blunt, so compelling. I did not realize it then, but what I was just introduced to was hope. I had known that I did not want Derrick to be swept up into a corner, but I did not have the answer as to how to prevent it. It was the title of this little book, *Needing You Even More*, which kept reverberating. Light dawned. This was a call to action. What a game changer – I was even able to think, "this might not be so horrible, Jane. It's gonna be up to you." Turning the booklet over, I saw a phone number for the Down Syndrome Society in New York City. Instantly I developed a plan – one I had no idea how to implement. But, I dialed the number and out of my mouth came, "I need 50 of these pamphlets so I can begin talking to new mothers of babies with Down syndrome. I am going to volunteer my services."

The Answer

I still had no idea of how to make sense of this new life with Derrick, but the idea of helping other mothers seemed to resonate. Back at the Brigham, I found myself heading to the same maternity ward I was on months ago. My mission? To speak to the RNs on the floor. "Remember you didn't know what to say to me when I had Derrick?" I asked. "Remember how helpless you felt? I want to be here for any new parent who gives birth to a baby with Down syndrome. Call me day or night, I beg you. I will be free. I work here 40 hours a week, but if I am not at work, I will drive in from the South Shore."

RNs and staff welcomed me with open arms, but only because I worked there. Not everyone who wants to volunteer in this capacity would be greeted that way, I would learn later.

Within weeks an RN called to say there was a new baby. I happened to be at work that day and, without really knowing what I was doing, I found myself in an elevator headed to the labor room. The scene is as vivid today as it was 35 years ago. I walked into the room and had to take a step back. There I saw it – me in that bed. The woman was sobbing uncontrollably. It was all a bit touchy. I first handed her the pamphlet from the Down Syndrome Congress and said, "Here is something to look at," and then offered my phone number. What came out next was, "I can tell you what I have done and what has worked." When I had her attention, I went on. "I kept phone numbers close by me, first for the Children's Hospital Clinic and then numbers of other mothers of babies with special needs." Though visibly distraught, she began to share a little. She taught at Boston University and told me that, at age 36, this was her first and only child. "I should have been tested," she wailed. "Why didn't I have that amniocentesis?" I ached for her. I left behind a copy of Edna Massimilla's poem. (I am happy to say that I ended up growing close to her and her child.)

The nurses at the Brigham soon asked me to put on a question and answer session for their obstetric RNs. "We had nothing to say to comfort you," they admitted. "We want to know first-hand how we can help a grieving parent." I am an open book, so naturally I answered, "Sure, I can do it, even with tears in my eyes." These meetings began with speakers discussing the psych issues – the guilt and the "why me" reaction. When it was my turn, I began by telling my raw story. "My husband and I had been married for ten years and didn't know if we were going to have children." I mentioned the endometriosis and the miraculous conception, and went on to describe the birth experience as honestly as I could. "I am the only one I know who screamed 'OH MY GOD, DOWN SYNDROME,' when he was less than an hour old. I felt like I created a monster." All the women, everyone in the RN class, gasped. There, I did it. I told the truth.

By the time I went to comfort the second mother with a newborn, the marquis in my head started to dim. For some reason each step I took seemed to bring *me* new strength. By sharing my story, I was able to give some hope. What I found was that each of them gave me the same gift in return.

With the common bond growing between us, I was finally able to say to mothers the encouraging words I longed to hear. "What you are feeling is temporary. This will be okay." I will never forget one young mother who pointed out, "Look at you, you're in a white lab coat, working full time, taking care of patients; your hair is clean, you have makeup on. Things have got to be good." And finally I was able to say, "Yes, life can and does go on. And yes, you can and you will smile again."

It would be two years before that screaming marquis in my head finally came down; and two years before all my fears and worries abated. Derrick is a baby first. He happens to have Down syndrome.

Earlier Days

I always wanted to help people, even as a child. At the age of 14, I worked as an aide in a nursing program changing bed pans, giving baths, even handing out medication. I loved it. Patient care was clearly a fit. I shifted gears at 16 and became a cashier; I could make more money, and needed it, for clothes and school things. My father, however, was very upset. "You have given up a nursing career to be a cashier." "No," I explained. "To be a nurse, I would still have to go to nursing school, it's not like it used to be." "What are you thinking? he screeched. A cashier doesn't go on to be anything but a cashier." When I eventually told him I was going back into a hospital, he was thrilled.

It was quite a fluke that while I was floundering on the wrong track in college, a fellow student in my economics class told me about the hospital training program in which his girlfriend had enrolled. "She's getting paid while training because there is a high need for these techs right now." I wasted no time filling out the application. Knowing the program accepted only five applicants a year, I badgered them until I was in. I trained at Children's Hospital and became an EEG tech. The Peter Bent Brigham Hospital, next door to Children's, recruited me while I was in training and hired me on the spot. I began in the Seizure Unit, which then became Neurophysiology. Once I saw all the instrumentation, I knew this was for me and was even more keen hearing that I would have to learn how to fix all the devices.

Our Second Child

Our new life with Derrick and Helen moved along, but Joe so wanted another child. I became pregnant by the time Derrick was 15 months old. We were enjoying being in our house on Cape Cod that summer. One evening, with Derrick in the stroller, Joe and I took a walk only to meet a friend, Kathy, who was out with her adopted baby with Down syndrome and her two biological sons. One of her sons asked, while peering into the carriage, "Wow, is his father Chinese?" "No, he's Down syndrome, like your brother Ryan," I responded. Derrick's slanted eyes, that epicanthic fold, was more pronounced than any other baby I had seen so it was not surprising that this little boy would be confused. "Someone's got to be Chinese," he insisted. I could feel his mother cringe.

There were plenty of awkward moments with people. As time went on I learned that humor can cut the tension. I am very aware of people who start to say something and then stop mid-sentence, unsure how to continue, fearful of how their next words might appear to me. Usually I finish their sentence with the words I know they wanted to say, adding a smile or even a laugh. Derrick was with me not long ago, going through the grocery line. The cashier totaled the order and as part of her script asked, "Would you like to contribute to the March of Dimes to help fight..." Looking at both of us, she came to a dead stop and quickly added, "birth defects." I answered, "I am living with one," and pointed to Derrick.

Clearly not everything was funny. I was still disassembling the marquis in my head and my pregnancy with Maryssa, while uneventful, was worrisome. And then there was Joe. He did have his years of drinking. Employed by the phone company's Install and Repair Department, most of his work was finished before noon so he met others in the trades at the local bar. He did this for years and years. While we were childless I did not think too much about it, but this day, a week before Christmas, I recall feeling not only overly pregnant with Maryssa but also frustrated and worried. Joe had said he would be home for supper, but it was now getting late. I was angry; actually, I was fearful that, like his sister Eileen, he would die from a freak accident – driving into a snowbank or off the road. I finally called him. "You started nagging me about this second pregnancy. You said that you still needed to know that you could have a normal baby and now you're out drinking? And you're going to be driving? You're going to leave me not only with a new baby but another one with a handicap? And neither with a father?" I was seething. Joe replied angrily, "You tell me right now if you feel I should stop drinking." "NO," I exclaimed, "you have to make this decision yourself. That is not going to be on me. You're not going to turn around one day and say 'Well, you made me stop.'" I hung up the phone. That was it, Joe quit drinking.

Amniocentesis, which was just coming about, almost killed my unborn Maryssa. If you were 35 or older and/or had a history of Down syndrome in your family, this test was recommended. Given the birth of Derrick and the fact that I didn't want to be catapulted into another state of grief, I went ahead with the test but learned later that there was only a one percent risk factor of having another baby with Down syndrome. Had I known instead that there were much higher stakes with this procedure damaging and even killing the fetus, I never would have had it done. Doctors performing an amniocentesis are supposed to stick the womb with a needle once, but during my procedure they went in and out so often that I started to have vaginal cramping and finally, when it was extreme, I screamed out, "Forget it. Stop. You are going to kill my baby. Enough." My husband, a Viet Nam vet, was backed into the corner of the room in horror. I was so traumatized by that experience that all through the night I kept waking to feel if I was losing her.

The day Maryssa was born, I felt nothing but pure euphoria. Not only had my OBGYN doctor listened to my concerns about this birth, but he took it a step further, calling Children's for a specialized pediatric doctor to be in the room with me so he could tell me immediately that the child did not have Down syndrome.

Joe is not a man of many words, but he was equally delighted with Maryssa's birth. As a kid, Joe was so involved in sports that I think he wanted to have a son who loved softball like he did; one who could hit a good home run and win trophies. Maryssa was never "Daddy's Little Girl," but he loved her deeply and never, ever, uttered anything derogatory about her being a girl. Joe, who felt as if his family was stripped away after the death of his sister and mother, reiterated all through the pregnancy that he would be happy with whatever we got. Had we been more stable financially at that point, I think Joe would have wanted to open the doors to adopting hordes of children.

Maryssa was a healthy, happy baby. She and Derrick fell instantly in love with each other. Everything was so different with her; she fed much faster and in a month had more neck control than Derrick did at nine months. It is not that I was looking for any of this or even comparing them every day, it was just that my experience with him was so fresh in my mind. None of this joy with Maryssa took anything away from Derrick. She was overjoyed with him and he adored her. She would smile at him when he came near, and he was always very gentle. Derrick was her "buba" (brother).

I kept saying I had twins, not as a complaint, just a fact. Their sizes might have been different, and she was on formula when he was not, but he too was in diapers and still took a bottle. I developed great upper arm strength from carrying the two around everywhere for years. Joe was also able to satisfy his sports enthusiasm by pitching buckets of balls to Maryssa and Derrick while I held their little hands around the bat and swung for them. At least they could get the idea.

Helen was there when Maryssa was born and continued to take Derrick to her house for the day. Even though Joe and I repeatedly said, "We can't pay you, Helen," she would still come over, do feedings and take Maryssa for walks, saying, "I want this baby to know me." Somehow, we scraped the money together to pay her. Maryssa to this day will tell you that "Auntie Helen was and is the best person I have ever known. I aspire to have even a fraction of the kindness my Auntie had and hope every day that she rubbed off on me." For me, Helen will forever have that halo over her head.

Show and Tell

I kept putting one foot in front of the other, visiting with new mothers and putting on the "How to Cope with a Grieving Parent" talks for Brigham and Women's RNs. In 1985, a neurologist at the Harvard Medical School, Dr. Bruce Korf, got wind of this support service and asked if I would bring Derrick with me to talk candidly with his first-year medical students about Down syndrome. I agreed, saying, "I will do this if you allow me to say what I want to say and not correct me. Don't forget, I am living this." I also mandated that they would not use or refer to the book, *Mongolism*.

Dr. Korf began the presentation by showing a few slides of children with Down syndrome, using some facts and pictures from the Pueschel book, *The Young Person with Down Syndrome*, published just the year before in 1984. Derrick was sitting on my lap watching the slide show when he started to hit his chest with one hand and point to the little boy with Down syndrome on the screen with the other.

When the show was over, Dr. Korf sat with us on stage and stuck a microphone in my hand. Students would ask anything from, "What do you think he will be able to do when he is an adult?" to questions about day-to-day life with Derrick, and on into queries about life expectancy and what my hopes were for him. This live "show and tell" was ground breaking for these medical students as information on this syndrome was scant.

It seemed like the only textbook for Down syndrome was that outdated book with sickly lime green lettering. In it they learned about a Dr. John Landgon Haydon Down, D.S., born in 1828 and who, by midcentury, became known for his description of a genetic disorder then called "Mongolism." In 1866, he wrote a paper entitled *Observations on an Ethnic Classification of Idiots* in which he put forward the theory that it was possible to classify different types of conditions by ethnic characteristics. Aside from Ethiopian and Malay types, he also referred to "Mongolian idiots." (How horrible for the people of Mongolia!) Dr. Down was able to proclaim these monumental findings as a result of his years as Medical Superintendent of the Eastwood Asylum for Idiots in Surrey, England. The first declaration was that people with Mongolism, Mongoloids, will look more like each other than their own family members and second, they will gravitate to each other. At that time, they even wondered if Down syndrome was a sub-class of human beings somewhere closer to the Neanderthals. It was not until 1961 in the medical journal, *The Lancet*, that the term Mongoloid was replaced with Down syndrome, named after Dr. Langdon Down.

So, in my early years with Derrick, I had people being taught (and believing) that my son's human development was closer to the ape. No wonder these medical students were in utter disbelief that Derrick could walk and talk. Many of them spoke up, asking why they did not have more classes based on people's experiences with these challenges. Soon the seminars expanded to include mothers of children with other chromosomal abnormalities. For a few years, I answered questions at these seminars, but between Maryssa's birth, Derrick's illnesses and a drastic change in hours that led to a new job at Harvard Community Health Plan, I had to bow out of that teaching commitment.

My name, however, showed up on a leaflet that Mass General Hospital sent to other hospitals. An article by Dr. Korf reached a doctor at Bexar County Hospital in San Antonio, Texas, who called to ask me to come and speak to RNs there. Joe did not want to go; he was not fond of flying for it appeared that every time he got on a flight someone in his family died. As a rule, I am not the one who wins out, but I arranged for my mother and Helen to watch Derrick and Maryssa while Joe and I went to Texas. In fact, we stayed three additional days to enjoy the city's fiesta season. It was probably the first time we were away without kids.

I began each of my two sessions with a video that showcased four parents raising children with Down syndrome at different life stages. After taking questions, I left them with phone numbers and information on the National Down Syndrome Congress.

More Medical Issues

Talking to others and being asked questions gave me an opportunity to reflect on life with Derrick. By this point I was learning that Derrick had a lot more intelligence than I thought. He also had a great sense of humor. My husband and I, with our sarcastic bantering, would often throw funny barbs around and look over to find Derrick laughing. How was this little child, much less one with Down syndrome, able to pick up that this was funny stuff? Today he can join in with the best of them.

Derrick could follow any conversation, but I became worried about his speech. "Ba-ba" was his word for everything. Fortunately, part of the Down syndrome program at Children's included evaluations with a speech pathologist. I explained that whatever word Derrick utters usually comes out garbled, and no amount of practice seems to change that. The pathologist told us he has an oral motor planning deficit. "His brain knows what he wants to say, but by the time it comes out it's muddled. It's similar to someone with a stroke." The pathologist simply left us with, "keep working with him." If he is reacting to something spontaneously, Derrick can be clear as a bell; and if something is very important he will make himself understood by either gesturing or describing the word.

We continued to learn things about Derrick, finding that he has his own peccadilloes; in particular, his eating habits. As he got away from formula, Derrick rebelled against most foods and only wanted pasta. He needed more nutrition, but because of the way he thrust his tongue when eating, he would push most foods out. At some point along the way it was suggested that I massage his facial muscles to help him process new food. I even found a special spoon designed to push the tongue down. But there were also unthinkable solutions, like the one a doctor gave me. "I don't understand why you can't just pour applesauce over whatever you are eating, and if he doesn't eat it in 20 minutes, just take the plate away." He was making *me* out to be the crazy one. I told him I could not do that, even asking, "Do you want to make my child a statistic for 'failure to thrive?'" He replied by asking, "Is this your problem or his?" I think this doctor was trying to make me cry.

At some point I heard about the Infant Feeder, a 4-ounce vacuum packed bottle with a wide opening in the nipple for feeding. It could also blend cereal with fruit. Twelve ounces of this thick mixture at each meal became his sustenance. There were more vitamins in this than in jars of store-bought baby food, which in those days was watery and loaded with sugar. Plus, I needed food at the ready. Derrick would often wake from a dead sleep famished, screaming and turning purple. I could not move fast enough.

I knew that children with Down syndrome usually had narrow upper airways, but it turned out that Derrick's soft palate was also very narrow with a high arch. When he ate French fries, for example, he would squirrel them away instead of swallowing them. He could mush them up, but he could not get them down.

Derrick also used to "crash and thrash," a term I used when explaining how Derrick slept. It was so descriptive that it eventually became the term ENTs used when diagnosing sleep apnea. Throughout the night he would thrash around, then he would sit up and bang his head into the side of the crib. I am guessing that even in his sleep he could not breathe well and sitting up helped him breathe better.

One day, around the age of three, Derrick fell asleep on the couch. Out of the blue, Joe shouted for me to come from the kitchen saying that there was something funny about the way Derrick was sleeping. Being in the business, I immediately saw a perfect case of sleep apnea. I called our ENT, Dr. Strom, the next day and told him that I had watched my son stop breathing. He immediately recommended a sleep study at Children's Hospital, which we were able to book for the following night. All through the test Derrick would tangle the wires as he thrashed about, and I would keep unraveling him.

Finally, at 5 am, the technologist came in and said the study was done. With results in hand, Dr. Strom reported, "He had good drops." I asked, "Good as in *good,* or good as in *significant?*" "Good as in significant," he said. Derrick stopped breathing over 500 times last night."

Dr. Strom theorized that people with Down syndrome would be more inclined to this problem because of the narrowing of their ears, nose and throat canals. (Derrick in fact, became a statistic for one of his papers.) To cure his sleep apnea, Dr. Strom proposed performing an adenoidectomy. That was fine, but he also suggested that he cut out his uvula and scrape both his palate and the back of his throat, which he likened to performing a "face lift" for the palate. We trusted this ENT, who had successfully placed a number of tubes in Derrick's ears over the years. Luckily, since this operation, Derrick has been fine. But, I thought, it is not bad enough that you are born with Down syndrome: you have passages that are problematically narrow; you have excessive mucus; you cannot swallow; and you stop breathing while you are sleeping.

Derrick's physical abnormalities were fixable, but I found that when I sought guidance for some basic issues, such as eating and speech anomalies, the process of finding a solution was like the blind leading the blind. There was never an easy answer. More often, I was just given suggestions, such as, "try this, try that." Seems we were all in the dark.

The Massachusetts Down Syndrome Congress

I soon learned that a group of parents from Massachusetts had looked into the National Down Syndrome Congress and then started a Boston chapter. It turned out that some of the Boston board members knew me because I had visited them after they delivered their babies at the Brigham. One of the members said, "Jane saved my life. She walked in with her own story and a fistful of information that I never would have known."

During the second year of the Boston chapter's existence, the president asked me to join the board and head up a statewide program to teach people how to be "support parents." We called this outreach group "Parent's First Call." Our mission was to touch base with the maternity ward administrators of all Massachusetts hospitals and explain the importance of providing support for new mothers of babies with Down syndrome.

Getting the program off the ground was slow and, I quickly learned, not easy. The Brigham knew us and welcomed us, but it was more difficult at many of the other hospitals where we did not have personal connections. Often I heard the staff say, "We don't need this, we love the babies all the same," which is when I would interrupt, saying, "This is not for the baby, it's for the woman who just had the baby."

Heading this project was exceedingly therapeutic for me. I could continue to teach doctors, talk to nurses and be there for the new mothers. We came armed with packets of information, guidelines and stories, but first we had to discern where each mother was emotionally. To prepare ourselves for these visits, we would role play various scenarios. For example, what would we say to a mother who told us, "I don't want anything to do with this baby; I don't like the way he looks." My answer was, "Okay. There are people out there who would be willing to adopt your child. So, if you really feel this isn't something you can live with, there are people who want him. It is considered the *adoptable* handicap." Hearing that these babies were wanted would frequently turn a mother's head around. "They're adoptable?" "People really want them?" They'd flip from, "I don't even know if I love them," to, "Don't take my baby away."

We worked hard anticipating new mothers' reactions to their babies, but we did not always safeguard against our own emotions. There were times, for example, when the support person would enter a distraught mother's room and burst out crying herself. I had to gather our group together and plead, "Please, think of yourself and what you went through. If you doubt, even for a second, that you can do these visits, please don't. We still need you, even if you don't interact with new mothers directly."

I learned to always first ask new mothers if they were going to keep the child. One devastated woman I encountered was a Harvard educated lawyer. I shared details about just how miserable I had been and tried to reassure her that everyone goes through periods of deep sadness. I went on to explain that she could always put her child up for adoption. She turned to me and said, "You know what Jane, I just don't think I am cut out for this." In the end, she gave up her baby. Out of the 40 or 50 mothers I spent time with, she was the only one who made that decision.

One couple I went to support presented an unexpected view. I began by telling them that this child could become the nucleus of their family, as Derrick had become in mine. The husband, an engineer, stopped me abruptly. "We are a family of five," he said. "I don't want a nucleus. Everyone is one-fifth a part of this family." This was my first challenge. He was so matter of fact that I did not have an answer for him.

Around this same time, in 1989, there was a new TV program called *Life Goes On*. It was an hour-long show about life in a family with a child, named Corky, who has Down syndrome. Within a few years of that show being aired, I would visit new parents and find they were not as hysterical as some of us had been just a few years earlier. Corky, played by Chris Burke, was a star in his family and to all who watched. He was competent enough to understand people and things around him, and bright enough to memorize lines, appreciate humor and get along with others. His character gave these newer parents the hope that most of us lacked early on.

It took four years, but we did manage to get into every hospital in the state. I felt tremendously rewarded by my role in the Massachusetts Chapter of the Down Syndrome Congress, but I stepped down after that.

Life Goes On

During those four years, Derrick and Maryssa began school. Derrick, at the age of three, went twice a week to a three-hour Pre-K program, riding an hour each way in a van. Helen would relay messages from the driver, and I had a communication book that went back and forth with his teacher.

One day the teacher sent a note saying she thought Derrick was ready for "big boy" pants. My first response was, "Whhaaat?" In my next breath I thought, "Allrighty then, if you want to try to train him, great, but I think he's years away from it." Maybe she had a plan to train everyone at once. I bought all the things the teacher asked for, but he really wasn't ready; it wasn't until the age of five that he got full control. (I vowed I would never tell a new parent this.)

His early program included all the basics one usually learns in Pre-K plus ADL (activities of daily living) skills and signing. I have observed that boys with Down syndrome are often much slower with speech, so learning to sign was a way Derrick could make himself heard. I was all for it.

In school, Derrick was actually mature for his age, thanks again to Helen. Her granddaughter, Hope, who was four when Derrick was born, was always asking her mother for a baby brother or sister. She was delighted to be his "little mother" five days a week; Derrick was the beneficiary.

Derrick soon went from two to three days a week in pre-school. While he was progressing on some levels, his speech was not. I asked for more speech therapy, but was told he was getting enough. At this same time, I realized I was more and more exhausted from my long, daily commute from the South Shore to Boston. Our only tie to living there had been Joe's sister, Eileen, and her husband, Billy, but by now Billy had remarried and moved closer to the city. Timing was perfect for a change.

Before we had kids, Joe and I lived dangerously and bought a house on a private beach on the upper Cape. It turned out to be a true thorn in our side. To pay for it we had to rent it, and the renters we had were awful. We never even lived there except the one summer I was pregnant with Maryssa. Because I was determined to increase Derrick's speech therapy, I considered moving to the town year-round, but quickly realized I would have to give up my job because of the impossible commute – which would leave me stuck at home all day with the kids. Joe's commute would have been even worse. The choice was made for us when I looked into the services the town offered and found they were even more limited than what we already had.

My thinking then went like this: If the current program is not going to give me what I want, how much do I have to pay in taxes to get what I need for him? We searched for two years and found the ideal community and the right lot to build on. We decided to sell our two houses for one, and moved in when Derrick was four and Maryssa was two.

They were great friends at that point and had a knack for getting into trouble together. One Saturday morning, just after we moved in, I woke to hear Derrick whispering the word "Hot." The two of them had gone into the spare room and plugged in the iron. Another day Joe and I found them standing in our mop bucket filled with ice cold water.

Our new address took away a third of my commute; our house was only two miles from the highway. Better yet, Derrick went from two speech therapies a week to four. It was the best of all worlds.

The town sent Derrick to a program in a nearby town. Derrick again had a long bus ride, but it was made clear that if he was the first one picked up in the morning, he would be the first to be dropped off in the afternoon.

Derrick attended the program happily and continued to make progress. He never had issues getting along with others as he had always been sweet; it did not hurt either that everyone thought he was so cute. Helen would now spend the day at our house to babysit Maryssa and be there for Derrick when he arrived home. When the program ended he, like his other six-year old classmates, went on to another program in a nearby elementary school, where he stayed until he turned 12. This was a significantly separate program with some integration, which was okay with me.

Justin Arrives

When Derrick was eight-and-a-half and Maryssa six-and-a-half, Joe and I added a second son, Justin, to our family. As part of my prenatal care, my doctor advised me to have an amniocentesis, which I vehemently refused. I told him that the test was senseless, because even if the results came back positive for Down syndrome I would not do anything anyway. "Well, let's not be heroic," the OBGYN said to me. Furiously I retorted, "I am already living with it, and if this child has Down syndrome my first born will have a companion for the rest of his life."

Justin was born healthy without amniocentesis in December of 1990. Within minutes of his birth I was prepped for a tubal ligation. The doctors tried to discourage me from having the procedure, saying that many women have children into their forties and that I may change my mind. I finally clinched the conversation by saying, "My first born was Down syndrome." They were stopped dead in their tracks. I see now that the finality of it all, knowing that I would never have another child, led me to dote on Justin a little more. I never thought I spoiled him, but I coddled him more than the other two. Justin was a colicky baby and would not stop crying. An older pediatrician had a theory: "When babies cry all the time and are under three months old, I tell mothers that it's colic. When they continue to cry after three months, I tell them, 'No I was wrong, you have a fussy baby.'" He went on to say, "I think with Justin, it's colic." Sure enough, at the three-month mark Justin stopped, but I still held him a lot.

People do not share much about how other sons and daughters in the family adjust to a sibling with special needs. It was a stigma then and may still be one. Maryssa never had a problem with Derrick's Down syndrome, but Justin was annoyed that he had an older brother

166

with special needs and took to ordering him around. I do not like admitting this, but Justin was a little tyrant. Derrick would be riding his adult trike and Justin, still with a binky in his mouth, would crack the whip, screaming, "C'mon, we gotta get the trash up the road." Justin would jump in the basket of Derrick's trike, throw the trash in and demand that Derrick pedal him all the way up the long driveway. Derrick did not like it, but he did it. I had never before seen a three-year-old making demands like a child dictator.

Maryssa disliked Justin because he was a bastard to her, too. He was cruel, taking her things and breaking them. Derrick and Maryssa both understood good behavior but Justin did not. Whenever Justin was reprimanded – even as a child – he would argue and yell, always having to be right and always having to have the last word. If I raised my voice over his, he would shout even louder. I recall my father saying, "First you yell, then your baby yells louder, then you start screaming and then Joe yells even louder. All the baby is hearing is you guys yelling." I actually thanked my father for saying that. We tried to be calmer after that and Justin did not scream as much, but he still had this sizzling personality that could explode on a dime.

How do I account for Justin's behavior? I can only speculate that the artificial sweeteners NutraSweet and saccharine, which were both in the gallons of Tab I drank when I was pregnant, are responsible for Justin's fiery temperament and his extreme case of ADHD.

In the early days, when I would come home from work, Derrick and Maryssa would have two hours' worth of stories picked out for me to read. As Justin became a toddler, I expected him to do the same, but he did not. I would pull the *Three Little Pigs* off the shelf to read, but Justin could not sit and listen for even a minute; he would be off telling me that he had to back the truck up to get the deliveries. He was two-and-a-half years old. I knew very early on that he would go to a Vo-Tech to learn a trade instead of tormenting himself in a college prep classroom.

As a youngster, Justin went immediately into a separate Pre-K program for "at-risk" kids. They took him based on the fact that he had a special needs brother. It worked for me.

Justin became an average student, but he was genius when it came to mechanical things. He was forever taking things apart and fixing them; he would repair kids' bikes in our driveway so often that it looked like we were having a huge bike sale. At the Vo-Tech he moved on to cars. "Let's put in new electronics, let's try new lights," he would say to his friends who hung out and watched as he worked. This routinely became an all-day affair, with 17 cars in the driveway, all with their hoods up. He was staying out of trouble and that was a blessing. Justin can do electrical, plumbing, tiling – anything mechanical. Today, he is a successful construction manager. He found his calling.

Trying Middle School

Similar to the medical issues I had encountered with Derrick, schooling for him was to be another maze. Derrick and his peers had spent most of their first ten years commuting rather long distances to programs in other towns. When they all turned 12 they were to go on together to a four-year program in yet another town. However, our town announced that they had just developed their own middle school program for kids with special needs so Derrick, they informed me, would not be moving on with his classmates.

I learned that the new class was to consist of four or five kids with learning disabilities who were included in regular classes but pulled out for tutoring. This left Derrick – the one and only student with Down syndrome – without peers, without friends, and…I would soon find out, without any type of individualized program.

This was inclusion. At first, I was happy to know that he was not going to be *in the room down the hall*, but then realized that maybe that is where he needed to be. I learned that inclusion might be great in the early years, but as time goes on, those with special needs are excluded more and more. I began to push back against inclusion.

Part of my hysteria when I first had Derrick was envisioning his life just like this: sitting alone in a program with kids throwing rocks, taunting him mercilessly and making mincemeat out of him.

The town was not able to convince me that this junior high program was adequate, but I was told I had no choice. When I refused to sign off on their plan, they basically said. "then you won't get any education for Derrick."

When I voiced my concern to other parents, they were incredulous. "Don't you want your son to graduate with his class?" I remember one mother, Martha, talking to me about her son Sam who had Asperger's. "Don't you want Derrick to get a diploma?" she asked. "Why?" I answered, "It's not going to help him. I want him to know how to wash clothes and go to the market." But Martha was hell bent on this piece of paper, despite knowing that Sam spent his school days throwing furniture around. Didn't she know that a simple piece of paper would not eliminate the issues? Maybe it would for her. Sam *looked* normal, so this would *make* him normal.

I scheduled meeting after meeting to no avail. My chief concern was that Derrick had no like peers. I was told to give the program time to prove it was not working. Unhappy with this response, I began my hunt for an advocate. I started asking around, calling people with children older than Derrick to ask for recommendations. The name Rocky kept coming up. I decided that even if I had to sign my weekly paycheck over to him, I needed to hire him.

I was reminded of a time when Derrick was little and I had gone into Boston to hear Emily Perl Kingsley, a trailblazer in the eighties. As a writer for Sesame Street, she was able to launch a new character, one based on her son who has Down syndrome. That day she happened to talk about "full inclusion." Using details from her own experience, she explained why it does not work. She described the elaborate parties that classmates threw, but neglected to invite her son. She went on, "We, in turn, had sleepovers, cookouts, campouts – you name it." The kids in his class would always come to their parties when invited because they were fun events, but not once did they reciprocate. And soon his "friends" were gone. She emphasized just how much her son needed his own peers. Jason was very high functioning; he even learned Hebrew and made his bar mitzvah. I couldn't believe *he* would be ostracized. Despite his accomplishments, his so-called "normal" friends still let him down. The truth is that the devastation happens to two people. The child suffers; the parent's heart breaks. Her talk stuck with me.

In the meantime, Derrick went to the junior high school every day, and there were interesting tales. Maryssa, still his greatest ally, was now in the same school and was able to give me snippets as to what was really going on.

Aside from having no peers, my other concern was what this program really looked like. Maryssa reported to us that his assigned teacher was not following through on tasks. For example, they would schedule Home Economics for Derrick. On laundry day, the job was to wash sheets and then put them in the dryer. Sounds fine, but one day Maryssa heard the teacher say, "Well, NO, the bell is going to ring, Derrick. We can't finish. You're going to have to move on." Maryssa saw Derrick look around the room, then run to the dryer, take the sheets out, run out of the room and down the corridor, still holding the laundry tightly to his chest. Before you knew it, there were teachers everywhere, chasing Derrick, who was halfway down the hall with wet sheets. This commotion prompted students to fly to their classroom doorways where they caught the spectacle and laughed uproariously.

In an effort to curb his seemingly head-strong behavior, teachers would say to Derrick, "If you're good today, we'll let you ring the dismissal bell." Maryssa explained that during one of her classes the school intercom switched on, and everyone waited quietly to hear what they thought would be an important announcement. Instead, they heard a distinct voice say defiantly, "NO, I'm ringing the bell!" After that, ripples of laughter burst out from every classroom. Apparently, Derrick had situated himself in front of where he thought the bell was but pressed the intercom button instead.

I also found out that aside from these obvious problems, the program was anything but thought out; it seemed to be made up as it went along. For example, his teacher would bring Derrick to the cafeteria to help, but the crabby women working there, through sheer body language, made it clear they did not want his help. His teacher was constantly having to invent "work" for Derrick. They would go to the office with him to see if anything needed to be done, or they would roam the halls. On these walks, Derrick would notice things that needed attention and alert the custodian to burnt-out light bulbs or unswept floors.

There was always a formal ed plan, but that focused almost exclusively on academics. I stressed that after 14 years of pounding the books, we had come far enough. "Derrick can bang on a calculator, he can tally things up and do math 'til the cows come home, but what he really needs is to learn to do a wash and fold it, go in and out of a grocery store, and cook a meal he'd eat on his own."

My advocate, Rocky, saw the program's failings clearly, but it took almost four years to document all the flaws. Maryssa was a tremendous help in advocating for Derrick. The school knew she cared deeply for Derrick; they asked her opinion often and liked having her insight as to what to do.

High School Challenges

Since our town did not yet have a high school program, we assumed that Derrick would follow along with the others who were in his previous class. They were all accepted into a nearby program run by a woman, Margo, who also happened to teach a summer school program that Derrick had attended. I had heard about the wonderful things Margo was doing in her high school program and had such high hopes. One student in her class was not only working at Stop and Shop, but also at a local gas station. He could read, speak well AND work. This is what we wanted for Derrick. It came as a complete shock to hear a flat out "No!" when we asked her about accepting Derrick into her fall program. Margo made her decision based on his performance in her six-week summer program. "That other program has ruined him," she said. "When you put him in full inclusion, he forgot how to interact with his peers." My heart sank, but I asked, "What is it that he's doing? Can you give me examples?" "He won't do what he's told," she answered. I asked what would happen if she rephrased things. She responded, "Oh well, he can be charmed, but we're not supposed to be charming him. He should just be listening to what we are asking and snap to." I asked her if I could quote her when talking to the special education director. She listed a few more things that would make him inappropriate for her classroom but her last comment almost cost her her job. She explained that he occasionally has to adjust himself and added, "I don't want any masturbation in the classroom." Margo did keep her job, but Derrick was still not admitted into her program.

With Rocky as my advocate, I went looking for another option. I knew there had to be another program, but after Margo's scathing assessment of Derrick I worried nobody would take him. Maybe, I thought, if we went in another direction, away from that town, we would find it. I was determined to have Derrick in a pre-vocational program.

Rocky found a school-to-work program at the North River Collaborative in Rockland. Despite it being out of my district, the town agreed to send Derrick. They even equipped him with what they believed he needed – a behaviorist. His last teacher from junior high insisted that Derrick needed to be rewarded every 15 minutes for good behavior. In the fall, shortly after he began in the North River Collaborative's program with his new teacher, Anne, she saw no need for the behaviorist and he was let go. Instead, she found that Derrick was a great candidate for this school-to-work program. "He was observant, determined and thorough from the beginning," she said. I saw the glistening halo over Anne's head and then saw her wings. I was thrilled that the Collaborative accepted him and that he would have peers.

Through this program, Derrick experienced various community training sites, not all of which were successful. He worked at a car wash where he soaked two employees. At a grocery store, he was told to get the carriages in the parking lot but was not mindful of oncoming cars. Each placement presented issues and I wondered where he was going to end up. I was open to anything and everything. He finally found his niche at a hospital in their "Stores" department, where he proved his competency for labeling medical supplies accurately and shelving them correctly. Over time he also became a whiz at filling and delivering orders and even remained at this job for a while after he graduated high school at 22.

Derrick had a good reputation there and was widely respected by fellow employees, but because of one instance, he was let go. On this unfortunate day, he was walking alongside his job coach to the elevator with his delivery cart. He heard the elevator door open down the corridor, walked away from the supervisor and ran to the elevator. That was the end. Despite the fact that Derrick knew what floor to go to and exactly what to do when he got there, the higher ups insisted on his dismissal. They said it was unsafe for him to be running down the hall, getting into the elevator alone, and allowing the door to close on the job coach. Derrick was merely showing his independence, but safety was the issue in their eyes; he was let go that day.

Life after Turning 22

We looked at different options for Derrick after he lost that job at the hospital, all of which were at "workshops" with a community job training component. Derrick was placed in a nearby day program where he tried out various jobs, including stints at both their bookstore and ice cream parlor, before he began working one day a week at a bottle recycling plant.

He loved it there, so I inquired about increasing the number of days, and soon he was working five days a week, from 10 am to 2 pm. It has now been 13 years and only one issue has been brought to my attention. Apparently, Derrick called one of his bosses "Honey" and put his arm around her neck. This boss, new at the time, felt threatened and registered a formal complaint against him. Administrators at his program had to act on it. Derrick was accused of sexual harassment and punished by being "temporarily relieved of his duties." Staff spoke to him about what he could and could not do in the workplace with male and female fellow employees, and he had to watch a movie on sexual harassment. Joe and I followed up by speaking to Derrick about the situation and asking if he understood what had happened. When he was allowed to return to the plant, his program staff cautioned him and re-iterated the rules every day on the way to work.

Derrick makes a few hundred dollars at work, which pays for some of his extra snacks: puddings, sodas and now, carbonated waters. We tried to get him off the diet soda, but it has taken years. We now buy him fizzy water, which eliminates most of the Pepsi. On a Saturday or Sunday, he will drink eight, two-liter bottles of sparkling water. Derrick lost 30 pounds when he stopped drinking diet sodas, even while he continued to gulp down a few of the sugared ones.

I can give Derrick a hundred singles at a time, and it will take him four to five weeks to go through it. I do not look in his wallet as he leaves every day, but I know that he takes four dollars to hit the soda machine. He drinks two sodas while he is at work and sneaks two more when he comes home. He thinks we do not know about this. He will stealthily come in the back door, quickly grab two cans and run them upstairs to the fridge in his room. Every day, Joe and I look at each other amused and say, "Oh no. Derrick's not home yet." Then he will come down, put his dirty thermos in the dishwasher and say, "How was your day?" as if he just walked in.

Derrick is quite competent in the kitchen. He knows how to place dishes in the dishwasher and can tell you everything that cannot go in it. On the weekends he prepares his own meals, beginning with oatmeal or cream of wheat with applesauce for breakfast, pasta at lunch and pasta at dinner. He makes his own pasta by boiling four quarts of water, adding the right amount of noodles, timing it precisely for ten minutes and carefully straining it over the kitchen sink. If he does not finish it all, he will try to fit the pan with the leftovers into the fridge; if there is not room, he will find the right Tupperware container. We always have a few Stouffer's in the freezer, and he is able to read the heating in-structions on his own.

I never have to ask Derrick, "Did you do this?" He has a clear routine in his brain and whatever needs to be done gets done. He keeps his bedroom neat, makes his bed daily and changes his sheets once a week. He nagged me last year about getting new sheets, pointing out a rip with one hand while handing me the newspaper insert for a white sale at Macy's with the other. He is persuasive, so I hauled him off to get two new sets. He chose plush ones – light blue and dark blue. The salesman who rang in the sale said, "You have expensive taste – 800 thread and satin! I can't even afford these."

Derrick is incredibly independent. I would not feel right about it, but I think he would be fine alone for a week. He does his own laundry to the point of argument, "MY laundry, MY soap." He needs to come with me to smell the detergents before deciding which one to buy. He even chooses what fragrance of Downy to use. He washes, folds and puts his clothes away with precision.

We do have different rules in the house; one we have discussed a lot is that you cannot wear anything with holes in it. I do not check his clothes since he has been dressing himself for years, but when we went to his doctor's office recently I looked down only to see huge holes in his socks. I was mortified. "There is no reason for this; you have whole drawers full of socks. Why would you choose to wear these on the day of your doctor's appointment?"

A couple of weeks ago I brought Derrick to his Monday night bowling league. Joe usually takes him and tells me how Derrick likes to be in charge by going up to the desk, getting his shoes, paying for them and, of course, keeping the change. That night he had spine, turning to me in the car and asking, "Well, where's my money?" I answered, "Have I ever brought you bowling and not given you money?"

Another Monday I brought him to bowling again since Joe was recovering from heart surgery. When Derrick was about to get out of the car he asked, "You're going to take me again next week, right?" I agreed and he added, "Okay, so then *you* will become the favorite parent" and walked off grinning.

As we were leaving the bowling alley, I looked at his polo shirt and saw gaping holes, which he tried to cover with his jacket. His friends and their parents had all come together to say their goodbyes, but I could not help myself. "What is the rule about the holes?" I shrieked. A fellow bowler piped up, "Oh my goodness, they look like moth holes." I was so furious I grabbed and pulled on one of the holes, completely ripping the shirt. Satisfied, I thought, "He will never do this again!"

Derrick was quiet in the car and threw out the shirt when we got home. It was not even a favorite shirt. I went over what I have said to him in the past. "Has mama ever said that you can't get something new? If you say you need something I drop what I am doing and we shop – we go wherever you choose and you get to pick out whatever you want, so why would you do this to me? It looks like mommy doesn't care about you." I believe I got through to him, but I think it took that kind of act. Since then, a few times he has proudly looked at me, pointed to his shirt and said with a grin, "No holes."

Joe took Derrick bowling the following week and explained to everyone that I was not out of my mind, but felt I had to make a statement. I am sorry if it was mean, but sometimes you have to go to an extreme with him.

Guardianship and the Future

At 35, Derrick is a grown up; he is responsible. My daughter has said she would eventually like to be Derrick's guardian. Taking on guardianship is a lot. It is one thing as a parent, but a sibling? I have comfort in it, but I am also attempting to be realistic.

Maryssa at 34 is mature and responsible. She is an Equipment Tech 3 in Mass General's operating room, and has risen through the ranks to the highest level, but she never saves any money. She insists that she does not want to be in patient care, even though getting her nursing license would double her salary. I have to stop nagging her. Maryssa loves the good things in life: travel, good food and eating out at the finest restaurants, but at this point she works two jobs to afford it all. She says she is content but I would love to see her enjoying her life with more free time. She lives on her own now, having just left a long-term relationship. I tolerated her boyfriend, who lived with us for six years, because I thought she felt this was the guy for her. I finally told her what I really thought and fortunately she listened but hated me for it.

If Joe and I were killed in a car accident, Maryssa and Justin would divide the proceeds from the sale of the house, giving Maryssa two-thirds of it since she would be caring for Derrick at least for an interim. Playing devil's advocate, I once said to her, "Maryssa, being responsible for a sibling with special needs has its difficulties, and life is hard enough. You had a boyfriend for six years and parted ways over different things, but what if you meet someone who isn't interested in caring for Derrick? Plus, you want kids and dogs – you want a life." Maryssa answered, "Well, if this boyfriend isn't in this with me, then he just wouldn't be the right person for me. I couldn't be in a relationship with someone who would be that shallow." Other parents have told me that none of their kids has ever said anything like this. One mother actually told me that her will stipulates that if her children are going to inherit anything at all, they must be involved with their brother's care.

Joe and I are Derrick's guardians now. When Derrick was about 23 his DDS (Department of Developmental Services) case manager interviewed him: "What would you do if you were sick?" and Derrick said, "I don't know." "Where would you go?" Again, he answered, "I don't know." There were several more questions where Derrick drew blanks (or chose not to answer), so Joe and I went through the legal process and obtained guardianship. I was told that at any point in time one of us could come off as his guardian and put Maryssa on.

A number of times I have requested that Derrick be put on a DDS list for group housing, with no results. My one concern about group living is that Derrick might lose the independence he enjoys right here. There are so many things he likes to do on his own, such as watching Red Sox games. Group activities might work well, but then again, he might not want to participate. Derrick has a system in place and he is happy with it. We, too, are glad he is a floor away.

It is funny how things have worked out. Thirty-five years ago, my hysteria came from thinking Derrick would be unsuccessful at anything. It also came from my father stressing that I had his curse and, deep down, I believed him.

Then there was the memory of that *room at the end of the hall*, the room I can still picture from when I went to junior high in Boston. It was hidden away on the second floor, where we were not even allowed to go. I do not remember seeing anyone with Down syndrome, but there were kids who looked different. It is awful to say, but I remember them coming out of their classroom and into places like the cafeteria, where they would have to sit, segregated, at their own table. All of this played into my depression in the beginning.

During the school's spring assembly, the entire student body would watch this group of students get their diplomas; though we knew none of them, we were told to applaud as they walked across the stage.

They shook the principal's hand and off they went, released into the real world. Our high school did not have a program for them; junior high was the end of the road for their education. The memory of how we made fun of them behind their backs was another big piece of my sadness. Thirty-five years ago, I was sure that God gave me Derrick to chastise me. I was terrified that people would point at Derrick and laugh. Worse still, I thought, nobody would want anything to do with him.

None of this is true today. I now understand that I was not cursed, and I was not punished. What I thought was my nightmare has been my greatest blessing.

Afterword

The five courageous mothers in these stories have overcome a multitude of challenges while raising their child with Down syndrome, and they have done it on their own. Their children were born on the cusp of important societal changes – in housing, education, medical and psychological needs, and social support services. Prior to the 1970s, those with "mental retardation" were institutionalized. Seeing their numbers rise and the cost to house them grow, federal and state legislation was passed to deinstitutionalize, creating a paradigm shift for society. It is only over the course of the last 45 years that changes began, and several endorsers of this book were ready for the challenge.

Remarkable people, such as Beth Moran Liuzzo and Dr. Patricia Maley, were forerunners in providing services for those with special needs. In 1978, Ms. Liuzzo, moved by the death of her beloved sister-in- law with Down syndrome, Lisa, entered the field of human services and helped to create the ground work for what she oversees today – the Brockton Area Office of the Department of Developmental Services. Over her 40-year career, Beth has overseen individual cases, has been responsible for the placement of people in various home and community settings, has trained specialized personnel, and has developed lifelong services for thousands of people with special needs.

Dr. Patricia R. Maley began blazing trails in the new field of special education, which began in 1972 with the federal passage of IDEA: Individuals with Disabilities Education Act. As an assistant director of a federally-funded grant program that year, she helped develop vocational skills for adolescent students with special needs. She went on to become a special education director, and later headed projects to provide early intervention to babies with special needs. Dr. Maley then served as the Executive Director of the North River Collaborative in Rockland, MA, from 1985 to 2005, and has been instrumental in creating dozens of programs for a wide range of people with special needs.

Deinstitutionalization and the subsequent growth of educational opportunities for this population indicate that we have made substantial inroads toward the original goal of "normalization," but significant gaps remain. For one, there are very few specialized practitioners in the medical and/or mental health field for this population. One such specialist in the Boston area is Dr. Florence Lai, a neurologist for over three decades affiliated with Harvard Medical School, Mass General and McLean Hospitals. Dr. Lai started a clinic for adults with Down syndrome in 1995, and has evaluated and followed hundreds of individuals with Down syndrome since then. Dr. Lai is currently involved in a National Institutes of Health research project to study adults with Down syndrome as they age.

Over a career spanning more than 40 years, Dr. Paul Schreiber, M.D., FAAP, has cared for more than a dozen people with Down syndrome. It is little known that pediatricians for this population often care for their patients through adolescence and into adulthood.

As for mental health care, specialized therapists competent to counsel people with Down syndrome and/or people with Down syndrome and mental health issues might be available in major hospitals, but are exceptionally scarce in our communities. Since 1980, Dr. Christopher White, Ed.D., has made a point to change that. Dr. White is one of the few licensed psychologists with advanced training in applied behavior analysis (ABA) and dialectic behavior therapy (DBT) on the south shore of Massachusetts. He has supported countless numbers of people with developmental delays. For the last ten years, Dr. White has served as President and CEO of Road to Responsibility, Inc., an organization providing residential, work/employment and day-hab programs, and other services, to people with developmental disabilities.

Life for children with developmental delays has improved over time, thanks to outreach programs through MDSC (Mass Down Syndrome Congress) and local ARCs (Association of Retarded Citizens). A relatively new program – Dads Appreciating Down Syndrome (D.A.D.S.) – has sprouted nationally and taken root in Massachusetts. The local chapter is headed by Jeffry Roback of southeastern Massachusetts, who is the father of two girls, Lilyana Grace and Allison Marie, and a son, 10-year-old Paul Miller, who has Down syndrome. D.A.D.S. of Massachusetts (www.dadsmass.org), which Jeffry began nine years ago, aims to assist and support, through fellowship and action, the fathers and families of individuals with Down syndrome.

The mothers who shared their stories in this book had children born in the dawn of deinstitutionalization, when services were being shaped. While headway in the areas of housing, health, education and family supports have been made, we are not finished. Hazel, Connie, Lisa, Ann and Jane's children are now adults and, as their mothers, they are again called to pave the unfamiliar way forward.

Author's Note

This book relies on each of the mother's personal experiences and memories as well as letters, photographs and legal documents. In certain cases, those source materials cannot possibly answer all the questions one might have. Some things remain unknown or forgotten and some things have changed since the writing of this. I have not invented anything; however, I did change a few names and locations to protect the privacy of individuals and institutions. These are the stories as told to me, nothing was embellished.

Acknowledgements

I can't say enough about these five mothers. They are extraordinary women who allowed me to write this book that, while my own, is really theirs. Before starting out, I told them I had no idea where their stories would end, but knew they had to be written. If there were doubts, I told them, I would shelve the project. But each of them told me to go ahead, "If it helps someone." They trusted me to write their story. I may never fully convey how much this means.

I am also so grateful to seven very special people who helped with the writing of this book. They, too, might not grasp the extent of my appreciation. I would like first to acknowledge Carlton Tucker, who has been there from the original iterations many years ago to the final ones. His discerning assessment, unwavering enthusiasm and light-hearted humor kept me focused and afloat more than he knows. Similar thanks to my two sisters, Mary Evelyn Tucker and Libby Tucker, who not only believed in my ability to finish this project but also offered reliable readership, thoughtful input and abundant support. Still close to home, John Grim and Kathleen Tucker cheered me on while my brother, Paul Tucker, and his wife, Maggie Moss Tucker, guided me with sage advice. It is to them all I owe endless thanks.

Along the way, I was fortunate to have had countless champions. I can no more find the words to thank these people than I can list their tangible and intangible offerings. Special thanks to: Cindy Blish, Jay Cole, Edie Coletti, Judy Cully, Eilene Davidson, Ginny Driscoll, Christiana Ferreira, Ann Marie Joyce, Jackie Leach, Michael Rogers, Pam Rudolph, Marcia Smith, Kathleen Staska, Carol Sullivan, Emily Uhl, Barbara Umbrianna and Annabelle Wallace. Add to this the many important connections at Seaside, as well as those in my other special groups.

As you can see, I had a lot of help. But going to print would not have happened without Henry M. Quinlan, my agent and publisher. Being a wise and caring soul, Henry saw the importance of this effort and was able to gently guide me through. And to Theresa Driscoll, my astute editor, thank you for making these stories read so effortlessly.

Last, but certainly not least, there is my husband, John, whose daily infusions of love have been unwavering. As always, they steady me and point me forward.

About the Author

Anne Tucker Roberts is a gifted teacher and writer. For nearly two decades she taught adolescents with developmental disabilities. After 12 years in this position, Anne was recognized as a Master Teacher and awarded a "Golden Apple" for professional excellence. Anne left this rewarding career to care for elderly parents. During that time, she began writing memoirs and completed two books. This book is the result of a new collaborative work between Anne and these remarkable mothers. Anne graduated from Boston College with a BA in Liberal Arts. She later earned a Master's in Education and a Master's in Special Education. She continues her work as a guardian to four women with developmental disabilities. She lives with her husband of 30 years in Scituate, MA.

Made in the USA
Columbia, SC
08 November 2018